HOW TO
GET SOMEWHERE IN THE
MUSIC BUSINESS

From Nowhere With Nothing

MARY DAWSON

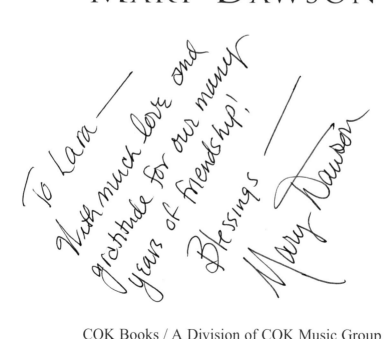

To Lara —
With much love and
gratitude for our many
years of friendship!
Blessings
Mary Dawson

CQK Books / A Division of CQK Music Group
Dallas, Texas

Published by CQK Books, a division of CQK Music Group. First printing, February 2007.

For information write:
      CQK Music Group, 2221 Justin Rd., Suite 119-142, Flower Mound, TX 75028
      Phone: 972-317-2760, Fax: 972-317-4737

Visit our website at **www.FromNowhereWithNothing.com** for many free resources and recommended services for songwriters and artists.

ISBN 978-0-615-13380-5

Book design and cover photo by Heather Dawson, ©2007Munkhaus LLC

To my husband, Dave, who loved me and shoved me outside my comfort zone.

CONTENTS

PART ONE
LEARNING THE BASICS
CHAPTERS 1-6

PART TWO

LIFTING THE BARRIERS

CHAPTERS 7-12

What's This Book All About Anyway?

How to Get Somewhere in the Music Business from Nowhere with Nothing is a response to the thousands of questions I have received from aspiring songwriters during my years as a music publisher, newspaper columnist, e-zine editor and host of my own radio talk show, *I Write the Songs*.

One day as I was typing the same answers to the same questions for the bazillionth time, I had a light bulb moment. It occurred to me that it would be easier to write the answers down one time in a manual or book so I wouldn't have to keep repeating myself. I invented an aspiring songwriter from the remote city of Boondocks, Montana. She asks the questions and I reply. This book will make a lot more sense to you if you keep in mind it was written as a dialogue.

As the book took shape, I found that it naturally fell into two sections. The first six chapters provide a basic introduction to the traditional music business and the last six chapters focus on ways the music business is changing in the twenty-first century. I decided to call the first part *Learning the Basics*, and the second part, *Lifting the Barriers*. Whether you are just beginning your music journey or have been at it a while, I trust you will find your own questions answered somewhere in these pages.

Rarely has any industry been so rocked by the winds of change as the music business has during the last decade. It would be difficult to exaggerate the size and extent of the transformation still underway or to fully anticipate all the new opportunities it is creating. Internet and computer technologies have radically decentralized the old power structure, opening a range of options to new and aspiring songwriters that were the stuff of fantasy just a few short years ago.

> *The basic thesis of this book is that it is absolutely possible to achieve (and even surpass) your musical goals—starting from where you are, with what you have—right now!*

How successful you will be depends on how willing you are to accept responsibility. Let me say that one more time:

> *Achieving your goals will depend on how willing you are to accept responsibility for your own musical destiny.*

If you'd like to keep writing and playing your songs, in the vague hope that Lady Luck will one day find you, you can save yourself some time and set this book aside. But if you're ready to stop dreaming and start doing something about your music future, you'll learn many things in this volume to get you started and keep you going down that sometimes bumpy, but often thrilling, path to success.

Mary Dawson
January 2007

Gratitude List

For years I have kept a personal gratitude list. It humbles me and sharpens my awareness of the many blessings I receive. The gratitude I have for those who contributed to the writing of this book could fill a book all by itself.

Here are just some of those people without whom this book would never have been completed: David R. Dawson—my editor, my friend and my firstborn. How did you get so smart?; Heather Dawson—your artistic eye and creative genius never cease to amaze me; John Dawson—you're like the cavalry, always coming to my rescue in the nick of time; Sarah Marshall—my music business sidekick, idea machine and constant support; Martha Gak—your prayers and love are the glue that has held me together; Si Simonson—for believing in me as a newbie songwriter and pushing me beyond myself; Kathy Womack—the angel who saved the day and the book when Murphy attacked.

THANKS to those who graciously helped us secure permission to quote respected sources: Dr. Allen B. Krueger, Dr. Koleman Strumpf, George Tobia Esq., Carol Harrington, Kimbe Malinek, Lynne Sheridan, Rose Marie Seminaro, H. Jackson Brown, Shannon Millard

THANKS to those behind the scenes who helped vet the contents of this book: Carol Guess Esq., Meredith Miller, John E. David Esq., Page Miller and many specialists at the US Copyright Office.

There are so many logistical challenges involved in writing a book like this one. THANK YOU to all who went above and beyond the call to bring this book to life: Don Mader, Dell Johnson, Rachel Nelson, Vicki Lindsey, Laura Ragan, Bill Millet, Gracie Hollombe-Vandiver, Jim Bingham, Sharon Jobe and Leo Dos Reis.

A special THANKS to so many greats in the world of music and songwriting who have encouraged me, spent time with me and treated me with dignity and respect—even though I might have appeared to be from Boondocks: Willie Nelson, Paul Williams, Richard Carpenter, Andrew Gold, Craig Wiseman, Ritch Esra, Jeffrey E. Jacobson, Esq., Jason Blume, Michael McDonald, Jim

Brickman, Carole Bayer Sager, Janis Ian, Bruce Greer, Beth Nielsen Chapman, Jimmy Webb.

This book would not have been written if it were not for the faithful support and friendship of those closest to me. Words cannot express my gratitude for all your encouragement during this process: Larry French, Lewis Greer, Rob Van Slyke, Beverly Houston, Kevin James, Marty Rendleman, Margaret Casey, Phil Paschke, John Kenward, Matt Pattillo, Peter Moon, Peggy Frank, Courtney and Al Delaney, Eulalia King, Sharon and Tom Braxton, Trey and Lynn Flesher, Dee Ann Nelson, Lisa Thomas, Joe and Ilene Strouse, Shirley Tidor, Albert Gak, Monica Dawson, Laurie Hanson Roberts, Jeanne Arnold, Robin Davis, Frieda Rothaus, DeRisa Payne, Molly Ragan, Banji Adebunmi, Frank Juma and especially to Clive, Daniel, Andrew and Lola—the "four under four" who keep everything in perspective.

Finally, at the risk of sounding cynical—which is certainly not my intent—I would like to thank all the people over the years who sent me rejection letters, refused to return phone calls, and in numerous other ways were unwilling to help me become an "insider." You forced me to become more creative, tenacious and resourceful in finding a back road up the mountain. It's been a little rocky but far more scenic than the wide, well-traveled highway you ran me off of.

PART ONE

LEARNING THE
BASICS

CHAPTERS 1-6

Square One

So, you say you're a songwriter, and you've written some pretty good songs...but you live in Boondocks, Montana, nowhere near a major music city like Nashville, New York or LA. You have little disposable income and absolutely no contacts in the music industry (except for your second cousin once removed who used to play third trombone in the VFW Marching Band). Are you doomed to obscurity? Is there really a way to get somewhere in the music business from nowhere with nothing? Where do you begin?

The answers to these questions are *no...yes...*and *right here and now*. Let's start at the very beginning—at Square One.

What Is A Song Anyhow?

This is really not as dumb a question as it may first appear! Every week I receive emails from talented people all over the country who want to be songwriters, but aren't even sure what a song really is.

A song comprises four distinct parts: melody, lyrics, harmony and rhythm. Melody and lyrics are a song's fundamental ingredients. They don't change. But harmony and rhythm may be changed to create different arrangements of the same song to suit the stylistic preferences of recording artists.

Consider, for example, how many versions of *Over the Rainbow* you have heard through the years. There is, of course, the original *Wizard of Oz* movie track version by the young Judy Garland, but then there is also the soulful Ray Charles version, the haunting Eva Cassidy guitar/vocal arrangement and Israel Kamakawiwo's Hawaiian rendition with ukulele. No matter how the harmonies and rhythms are changed, the song remains the same. It's still *Over the Rainbow* because each arrangement has the same words and melody.

Don't Some Songs Have Just Music? Or Just Lyrics?

Of course, we all know beautiful songs that have no lyrics—jazz and classical compositions especially. These songs are often performed and recorded (at least initially) by their composer(s). Jim Brickman's popular piano compositions are a beautiful example, as are jazz classics by a host of artists from Duke Ellington to Wynton Marsalis and all points in between. Other instrumental songs gain popularity because they are written for films that become blockbuster hits—songs like *The Pink Panther*, or *Tara's Theme* from *Gone With the Wind*. In recent years electronic music has become another very popular type of instrumental. House, dub, trance, downtempo, and ambient electronica have become hit musical art forms. All instrumentals may be registered as songs with the US Copyright Office, a department of the Library of Congress.

Stand-alone lyrics may also be copyrighted as songs but the opportunities that exist for lyrics without music are extremely limited.

What Is A Songwriter?

For the purposes of this book a songwriter is someone who writes compositions with words and a melody. Someone who only writes lyrics is a lyricist. Someone who only writes music is a composer. To be a writer of songs, your compositions must comprise both words and a melody. Harmony and rhythm are optional.

What If I Only Write Lyrics?

One of the most frequent questions I receive from hopeful writers and poets around the world is this: "What if I only write lyrics? Can I still break into the music business?"

My answer to this question is difficult to give, but it's always the same. Your chance of breaking into the music business as a lyricist only is slimmer than that of winning a million lutfisk a year for life in the Swedish lottery!

Songs are the commodities of the music business. Trying to break into the music industry by writing only lyrics is like trying to break into the shoe business by making only right shoes. Shoes are sold in pairs. Songs pair words with music.

A musical composition without words may succeed as an instrumental, but words without music are mere verse. As the old saying goes, "You can't whistle a lyric."

What If I Don't Play A Musical Instrument? Is There Any Hope?

If you only write lyrics, whatever you do, please don't stop reading here. There is hope! First, you may consider learning to play an instrument…just enough to compose a melody. The famous Johnny Mercer, writer of over a thousand songs, was known as a great lyricist, but he also wrote melodies on occasion. How? By thumping them out with one finger on the piano. You needn't write an entire arrangement—all you need is a melody to go with your lyric.

You would be amazed at how many extraordinarily successful songwriters do not read or write the first note of music. Academy Award winning songwriter, Paul Williams, once told me that early in his career he had to number the piano keys with a magic marker in order to tell one from the other. Some of his greatest songs were written utilizing that method. The simple fact is you don't have to be a trained musician to be a songwriter.

But, what if you don't even have a melodic idea? Then what? There is hope yet. The answer is collaboration. Johnny Mercer's list of co-writers reads like a *Who's Who of Tin Pan Alley's Most Famous Composers*: Hoagy Carmichael, Harold Arlen, Vernon Duke, Jerome Kern and dozens of others.

> *The moral here is that if you take the craft of lyric writing seriously, you will find musicians who are delighted to collaborate with you. When you have both words and a melody, you have something that just might be of interest to the commercial music industry.*

Where Am I Going To Find A Collaborator?

The answer is, "Anywhere you can."

We will have more to say about the importance of your nearest local songwriters' organization a little later on, but if you can find a group of songwriters in your area who meet regularly—that will be your first and best resource. There you will be able to find writers of all skill levels who are serious about learning the craft of songwriting and enjoy collaborating with each other. The atmosphere is non-threatening and friendly—a great place to begin. If, however, you are unable to find a songwriters' group, there remain other promising possibilities.

First, start getting out more. Get in the habit of perusing the *Arts and Entertainment* section of your weekend newspaper. Become familiar with the hot clubs and coffee houses in your area where local singer-songwriters may be appearing. Consider visiting the music department of a local college or university—or even a large church. Make an appointment with the head of the department and introduce yourself as a lyricist who is looking for collaborators. You might even put a notice on the department bulletin board. From that point on, it's a little like dating. Extend yourself, try a co-write or two with someone else and see if anything clicks. You may have to kiss a few frogs on the way, but you will eventually find the right connection and songs will start flowing. It's a little scary, but fun—and very rewarding.

What About Finding Co-Writers Over The Internet?

The Internet has of course opened many doors to songwriters. Websites catering to aspiring songwriters and artists allow people from all over the world to hear each other's music and offer feedback or critique one another's songs. It's a large cyber fellowship! If you choose to become part of one of these sites, you will discover talented people with whom you may co-write without ever having a face-to-face meeting. File sharing and web conferencing options are much like being in the same room writing songs the old fashioned way.

One of my favorite co-writers is Sal Anthony, a talented composer/artist from Pennsylvania. We met several years ago through *Songlink,* an Internet publication that originates in Europe (talk about a shrinking world). Sal had placed a classified ad for a lyricist and I responded. We began getting to know each other. He sent me samples of songs he had written and I sent him samples of mine. After some time we decided to try writing a song together and found we were compatible. It was easy to communicate with Sal and I found him very fair and honorable—a genuinely nice guy with a wonderful talent for writing amazing melodies.Though Sal and I have never met in person, we are the best of friends and have collaborated on many songs that I am very proud of. Check out Sal's music at **www.SalAnthony.com**.

Meeting people online is like meeting people in any public place. Be cautiously friendly until you really get to know someone. If the relationship starts to feel uncomfortable, withdraw. If you begin to click with the other writer, you may be about to write some wonderful new songs.

Just a word about the many Internet songwriting forums and chat rooms that exist today. While they can be wonderful places for beginning songwriters to meet each other, ask questions and learn from those with more experience, be aware that they sometimes generate a good deal of misinformation. Many discussion threads veer incrementally away from the truth with each new authority that weighs in. As in a game of telephone, what began as a fairly accurate statement may end in total confusion. Contributors may or may not post accurate information on important subjects like copyright ownership and the business of music. Unless you are absolutely confident of your source, never substitute Internet chat for books by established professionals or consultations with an experienced entertainment attorney.

Is It OK To Pay Someone To Write Music For My Lyrics?

Shark Warning

When you surf the Internet or browse music magazines you are likely to see advertisements for services that offer to set your lyrics to music for a fee. Approach these with great caution. Some are legitimate but many are not.

Bogus music companies often have enticing websites. They may claim to be located in "the heart of Music City" or on the Avenue of the Stars in Los Angeles—right across the street from Warner Brothers or RCA. (FYI…There are dumpsters in those places too.) They may boast of brushing shoulders with music executives every day in the office elevator (so does the janitor).

You get the idea…while some of these claims may be true, technically speaking, they have often been exaggerated to entice unsuspecting songwriters—especially those who live far from the music centers and tend to be more easily dazzled by high profile names and places.

Such companies eagerly solicit "songwriters at all levels—even those who write lyrics only." If you send your lyric or song to them, they will usually follow up with an extremely flattering response complimenting you on your songwriting ability and offering you a smorgasbord of services from melody writing to demo production—and even publishing and promotion—all of which, by the way, you are expected to pay for.

If you are even considering doing business with one of these outfits, be sure that there is a written agreement you understand completely. Listen to your gut and beware. There may be sharks in the water!

Finding Legitimate Production/Composition Services

While I have never personally solicited a production company to create music for my lyrics, I receive inquiries every day from lyricists looking for good melody writers to complete their songs. They are often having difficulty finding someone to collaborate with locally. In an effort to steer them in the right direction, I have discovered a number of legitimate services. It is each songwriter's responsibility to research her options carefully.

Reputable composition/production services don't usually charge for the music they create Instead, they will enter into a co-writing agreement with you so that you share equally the ownership of the completed song. Because the composer or production service has been specifically solicited by you, the lyric writer, to create music for the song, you will usually be charged for the demo production. But if the song begins to generate income, your demo production costs can and should be recouped from the earnings before any future profits are divided between you and the production service as the co-owners of the song.

One of the best and most reputable demo production services I know of is *The Songwriters Studio* in Nashville. I have personally worked with producer Steve Cooper, for years and have referred many aspiring songwriters to him—especially those writing country, folk or Christian Contemporary songs. I have never had anyone express displeasure with either Steve's work or his ethics.

For information on production services, we recommend a visit to our website at **www.FromNowhereWithNothing.com**.

Any Suggestions For Music Writers?

Your strong suit may be classical or jazz composition, but there is no reason you can't master the art of writing hit commercial music if you feel so inclined. Another of my favorite collaborators, Cheryl Bocanegra, holds a Ph.D. in Music Composition and Theory. But she can write a heck of a country melody!

There are many wonderful tools and services listed in the resources pages of our website at **www.FromNowhereWithNothing.com**. You will discover books and even entire songwriting courses to help you learn the craft of commercial songwriting. One of the best is the online songwriting series available through Berklee College of Music—especially the *Songwriting Workshop Series* by Jimmy Kachulis, Professor of Songwriting.

If you decide to write songs, you will, of course, require lyrics. You may wish to study the craft of lyric writing yourself, or you may decide to do a little undercover work to find polished lyricists in your community desperately looking for collaborators like you.

Anything Else?

We will, of course, have much more to say about songs, songwriters and co-writers throughout this book—especially in chapters five and six where we will examine the very important business aspects of music and the pleasures and pitfalls of co-writing. But you already know enough to get started. Begin by doing a face-the-music reality check of your songwriting abilities. Admit your weaknesses and identify your assets. Then take one step this week—no matter how small—to improve yourself.

Whatever you do, keep networking…reaching out…finding other writers…stretching yourself…trying new things. I promise you, you have brain cells you have never even begun to use.

Whether you are a lyricist or a composer or both, just remember: A commercial song must have both words and a melody. You can come up with both, either on your own or in collaboration with others. Do it!

REWIND...

~ A songwriter is someone who writes songs—compositions with both words and a melody.

~ If you can't write both, either learn to do so—or find collaborators to help complete your songs.

~ Take advantage of the many legitimate resources available to help you get started in the craft and business of songwriting.

Beware of sharks!

NOTES

2

Do-It-Yourself Publishing

What Is A Publisher And What Do They Do?

Now that you are busily writing songs and finding co-writers to work with, you may recall hearing somewhere that writers need music publishers to help promote their songs. But you're not sure what a publisher is or does—or even what a publisher looks like. Do you really need one? The answer to that question is both *yes* and *no*. Yes, you definitely need the services of a music publisher. But if you don't have access to one, you can be your own publisher. To find out how, read on!

Music publishing started as far back as the printing press. Entrepreneurs who owned presses would create all kinds of printed merchandise—calendars, magazines, posters and books—to be sold by salesmen who carried these items to small towns and cities. A songwriter often arranged with a printer to print copies of his latest composition as sheet music to sell with other items. The printer and the songwriter would then split profits. That arrangement was the rough draft of the publisher/writer relationship that still exists today.

Basically, a music publisher is the real estate agent for your song. Like a realtor who arranges with a homeowner to sell a house for a percentage of the sale price, a music publisher contracts with a songwriter to exploit the earning potential of a song for a percentage of earnings. Neither the real estate agent nor the music publisher is absolutely necessary! Homeowners can sell their own houses and songwriters can promote their own songs. The advantage of having a realtor or a publisher is that these professionals bring all kinds of expertise and many contacts into the equation—expanding potential profits for everyone.

Before we examine the options available to the songwriter for music publishing, it will be necessary to discuss the very important matter of copyright.

What's The Scoop On Copyrights... And Wrongs?

When I first began my journey as a songwriter, the very mention of the word *copyright* provoked a feeling that was equal parts mystery, awe and paranoia. On one hand, horror stories about song stealing, and lost fortunes underscored the importance of ensuring my songs were protected by law. On the other hand, the word *copyrighting* bespoke bureaucratic complications and miles of red tape. I was quite overwhelmed every time I paused to consider it! For a long time, I simply ignored the whole matter and hoped it would go away. It didn't. If I had known then what I know now, I would have realized that the word *copyright* is kinda like the word *eggplant*. It sounds pretty scary. But when you try it, you find it ain't so bad after all!

> *Copyright is the exclusive right to copy, reproduce, publish and sell literary, musical or artistic work.*

In music biz vernacular, the word, *copyright*, is often used as a synonym for the word, *song*, because whoever holds the copyright owns the song. The good news is that you really don't have to do anything except write a song in order to be protected by copyright law. It goes into effect automatically the moment the expression of an original idea becomes *fixed* in a tangible form or medium—such as written lyrics, transcribed notes on music paper, lead sheets, audio recordings and the like.

The key word here is *fixed*. As long as your song is simply floating around in your head—a melody you sing in the shower—it has not yet taken on a tangible form. Until it is transcribed on paper or recorded, it is too hazy to be formally protected.

> *The moment the ink is dry—and/or the words and music are recorded on tape or CD—the song is owned solely by the writer(s) and is automatically protected by copyright law for seventy years after the writer's death! When there are two or more writers, copyright protection extends to seventy years after the death of the last surviving writer.*

The correct way to show ownership is to print the word *Copyright* or the letter C in a circle © followed by the year the song was completed and the name(s) of the writer/owner(s). This notice should appear on everything that has anything to do with your new song—lyric sheets, lead sheets, working cassettes and demo recordings. Be sure that it also appears on any lyrics or MP3 files you send over the Internet. It will look something like this:

©2007 / Mary Dawson

Novice songwriters can be a little paranoid about the protection of their creative work. You can relax if you have properly marked everything with the copyright notice I've just described. Your songs really are protected and most music industry professionals know that. Nevertheless, when you begin to get airplay or should you begin pitching your songs to a wide variety of publishers and record companies, you are well advised to register your copyrights with the US Copyright Office in Washington, D.C. Do this especially if you send your songs out regularly over the Internet.

For complete details on registering copyrights refer to Appendix A in the back of this book.

To Summarize

The copyright is the *deed* for a song. The writer or writers automatically own the whole song from the moment the words and melody are fixed on paper or in a recording. If and when you choose to enter into a songwriter's agreement with a music publisher, you will surrender the ownership or the deed of your song to the publisher with the understanding that she will share any future income from the song with you. We will have more to say about songwriting agreements in chapter five.

What Exactly Is Do-It-Yourself Publishing?

If you have written a song or songs, you are a copyright owner. Until you sign an agreement with another publisher, you remain the sole owner and the *de facto* publisher of your own songs. I know you may not have signed up for this job, but it is yours by default, so let me be the first to welcome you to the wonderful world of DIY Music Publishing.

The Two Hats of a Publisher

A music publisher:

   1) *Promotes songs* by seeking to maximize their circulation, impact and financial profitability.
   2) *Coaches and mentors* promising songwriters.

Song Promoter

The first hat the music publisher wears is that of song promoter. Since the publisher's entire business is music, she has a wealth of contacts and experience that can enhance the likelihood your songs will earn money as print music, recordings, videos, media performances, and commercials. She may even help develop your song's potential for foreign sub-publishing. A knowledgeable and energetic music publisher who believes in your songs can be an invaluable ally in getting them to the world.

But music publishing ain't rocket science! If you don't have a publisher, you can learn how to do it—and do it well. It will require a basic knowledge of the business, lots of trial and error and Herculean tenacity, but it is do-able.

COACH/MENTOR

The other hat the music publisher wears is that of coach and mentor. A songwriter who writes exclusively for one music publishing company (a staff songwriter) has a great advantage in that she has personal access to the expertise of the publisher (who may also be a songwriter) for feedback on the songs she is creating. The publisher can further arrange for a writer to collaborate with other writers who are stronger in certain aspects of the craft. This cross training is a serious boon to the development of a writer's talent. Good publishers—like good coaches—can pull the maximum from those they mentor. I am eternally grateful to a wonderful publisher who took an early interest in me as a beginning, diamond-in-the-rough songwriter and pushed me out of my comfort zone to make me a better writer than I ever dreamed I could be.

What Do I Do First?

In a nutshell, you will have to begin by wearing both of the publisher's hats. We'll discuss the first hat—that of the promoter—in later chapters of this book. The second hat—the hat of the coach/mentor—can be donned immediately. You, the songwriter, can become your own coach and begin realizing your maximum writing potential.

What Are Some Practical Steps I Can Take To Mentor Myself?

Develop a Disciplined Reading Program

Contrary to what many may think, songwriting is not just a matter of being suddenly inspired and writing a worldwide hit during your lunch hour. Sometimes that does happen, but it usually happens to those who have spent months and years learning and polishing their craft. Like any other skill, songwriting requires a mastery of the tools of the trade and the rules of the craft.

The first thing any serious songwriter can and should do is begin a reading program on the subject of the craft and business of music. Make a date with yourself next Saturday afternoon and take a leisurely trip to your local bookseller. Grab yourself a cappuccino and browse through the many wonderful books on songwriting in the music section.

FOCUSED READING

Become familiar with songwriting authors and titles, then develop a focused reading program. Many years ago Waldron Scott, a brilliant and extremely well-read gentleman, shared with me his personal reading regimen—one I have adhered to ever since.

He began by reminding me that once you are out of school and away from a structured curriculum, your continuing education is your own responsibility. No one is going to assign a book for you to read and report on. There will be no exam dates or term paper deadlines to keep you focused. You must discipline yourself!

He suggested reading a specific number of books as an objective for the year. Consider your time and be realistic. You might, for instance, set as your goal to read twelve books—one a month. Design your reading program topically. If six of those twelve are about songwriting, at the end of one year you will have learned much about a skill you intend to acquire and perfect.

You may choose to design your reading program around specific skills, such as melody creation or lyric writing. Or you may choose to explore various aspects of the business of music. You may even decide to read biographies of great songwriters and study their songs. Whatever you choose, stay with it—just as if you were taking a course for college credit. Do what it takes to stay on schedule.

THE PROCRASTINATION PROBLEM

Are you a bit of a procrastinator? Not a great self-starter? You may want to build some accountability into your reading program. If you are in contact with other songwriters in your area, you may decide to tackle your reading list together and have monthly discussions about what you are learning. Or you may simply set yourself a deadline for completion of each book and write a short book report on your computer to document that you have actually finished it. It will not be long before you will be as knowledgeable about the various aspects of songwriting as anyone else in the business.

FACING FINANCES

Now, I realize that books can be very expensive and that few aspiring songwriters can go out and purchase an entire songwriter's library all at once. May I suggest that you start your collection with a good beginner's text (like John Braheny's *The Craft and Business of Songwriting*)? Then, when you have a birthday or when Christmas is coming (or Valentine's Day, Mother's or Father's Day, Groundhog Day—whatever holidays you can squeeze a gift out of) ask for another book! It will make gift buying easier for your loved ones, and instead of another ugly necktie, you'll have something that advances your songwriting career.

And while we're on the subject of money, it's not too soon to let you know that this songwriting habit we are all addicted to is going to be pricey. Building a good songwriting library is only the beginning.

Many songwriters write to me with dreams of making it in music, but are unwilling to part with the first dollar to begin their journey. Fantasies of some flashy music cash cow appearing out of nowhere to finance a music career fuel this miserly mentality. Try to think of it this way:

> *Any hobby—golf, photography, scrapbooking or whatever—is going to involve some expense. The more involved you get and the more adept you become, the more expensive the hobby is likely to be. If you love what you do, however, you will find a way. You will sacrifice other little luxuries; you will create a budget; you will fund your avocation somehow, some way.*

The same is true for the craft of songwriting. While there are many ways to save money (you'll find lots of suggestions in this book), there will be costs. Your music library is just the first of many expenses you will have to absorb. But books are essential. If you want a successful songwriting career, they are worth every penny you'll spend on them.

Remember: No matter how gifted you may be as a musician or lyricist, you are also your own coach/mentor/publisher. Wherever you live, whatever your level of musical or lyrical skill, you are only as far away from growth and help as you are from your nearest bookstore or local library! Discipline yourself to read!

For a list of books that I recommend to every serious songwriter, visit our resource pages at **www.FromNowhereWithNothing.com**.

So I'm Reading Already...Now What?

Exercise for Excellence

A good fitness program involves more than the proper intake of nutrition. It includes vigorous physical activity. Reading books may be good nutrition, but it is just as important that you start writing. This is the workout portion of your program.

One good way to workout is to simply complete any assignments and exercises that may be included in the books you are reading. But remember, a publisher also mentors her staff songwriters by setting them up to collaborate with other more experienced writers from whom they can learn the fine points of the craft. If you are acting as your own publisher, you must do this for yourself. Here's how:

1. Compile a List of 8-10 Classic Hit Songs

I'm thinking about songs such as *Over the Rainbow* by Yip Harburg and Harold Arlen. The National Endowment for the Arts and the Radio Industry Association of America declared this song the Greatest Song of the Twentieth Century! Or how about a great Beatles song like *Yesterday* by Paul McCartney, that has the honor of being one of the most played songs ever in the United States. Or, if you are a little more advanced, you might consider one of the amazing songs of Burt Bacharach and Hal David such as *Promises, Promises* with its irregular meter and creative phrasing. You get the idea, right? Your list should be thoughtfully compiled and extremely selective.

2. Set Up a Collaboration Appointment

Your next step as publisher is to set up a collaboration appointment for yourself with the great writers who wrote the songs on your list. Now, I can just hear you saying to yourself, "How am I ever gonna collaborate with Sir Paul McCartney?" or " Yip Harburg and Harold Arlen are even more out-of-touch since they have both passed on to that great Recording Studio in the Sky!"

Before you write me off as one taco short of a combination plate, just finish reading this section.

3. Eliminate the Lyrics

First, throw out the lyrics of one of the songs on your list, and write your own lyrics to the existing great music. Your lyrics should tackle a completely different subject or idea, but make sure they are appropriate to the style of music under consideration. Take time with your new lyrics. Make your rhymes appear where they do in the original song. Be sure that the stressed syllables are also the same.

4. Eliminate the Melody

Once you have your new lyric finished, reverse the process. Write your own music to the original lyrics. Stay true to the message of the song when you write your melody. Don't take undue liberties. Try to discover the techniques your collaborator used.

Be aware that you cannot legally replace either the words or the music of any song that has been copyrighted. But once you have written a new set of words and a new melody to the template that exists in the song, you may then combine the two parts to create a completely new song. You will find that you have learned volumes from the wonderful collaborators you are writing with.

Attend Songwriting University

Every good music publisher encourages staff songwriters to attend workshops and classes on the craft of songwriting. Unfortunately, many of these workshops are offered in the big three music capitals—Nashville, New York and Los Angeles—and there you are, stuck in Boondocks! But the good news is that songwriters everywhere have at their fingertips a virtual University of Songwriting in a simple electronic device: the radio.

Songs of every style float through the airways and are accessible to every writer who wants to learn—even to those who live on the backside of Nowhere.

Legions of Grammy Award winning songwriters have testified that their best teacher in the craft of songwriting was—and still is—the radio.

But there is a catch! You can't just "veg out" and listen for sheer enjoyment. Train yourself to listen critically. Ask yourself:

♫ *What kind of song is this?*

♫ *What is the hook?*

♫ *Does it have a chorus?*

♫ *How are the music and lyric writers setting up the chorus to make it pay off and become unforgettable?*

♫ *What musical sequences, modulations and other techniques are being used?*

After you have heard a hit on the radio, try picking it out on your instrument. Find the chords. Write a new melody to the basic chord progression. You are now attending Songwriting U.

Push yourself a little! Don't just listen to songs in genres you naturally enjoy. I recommend that every button on your car radio be set to a different style of music – Country, R&B, Pop, Alternative, Rock, Jazz, Classical, Christian Contemporary etc. As you station surf in your car, listen and learn from the greats in every genre. Some songs will be in genres you don't care for, but if they have sold tens of thousands of copies, there is probably something you can learn from them!

CONCLUSION

So there you are….still in Boondocks. But you are already starting to get somewhere by acting as your own publisher. There is no way that you can follow the suggestions in these first two chapters and not improve as a songwriter. And the more you improve, the more difficult it will be to "hide your light under a bushel." Eventually, somehow…some way…excellence finds a way to rise to the surface.

The ball is really in your court. How hungry are you to be a great songwriter?

REWIND ...

~ A copyright is a business synonym for the word, "song". Every songwriter is protected by copyright law from the moment a song is fixed in an audio or printed medium.

~ Music publishers wear two hats:

    Promoter for the songs

    Mentor for the songwriter

~ Do-It-Yourself music publishing begins when you take responsibility for mentoring yourself as a songwriter through:

    A Disciplined Reading Program

    A Writing Exercise Program

    Attending Songwriter's University
    (listening to the radio)

3

The Demo

You can always tell when a songwriter is composing a new song. She has an unmistakable glassy-eyed appearance. The lights may be on but the writer isn't home (if you know what I mean). You may observe lips moving in wordless mumblings or fingers tapping out syllables. Whatever the outward symptoms, they are sure signs the songwriter is hearing something the rest of us aren't.

And therein lies the need for the songwriter demo.

> *The demo lets the rest of the world hear the song that has been playing in the songwriter's mind for days or weeks. The demo helps the rest of us get onto the songwriter's wavelength and share the emotions that inspired the song.*

On a business level the demo is essential if the songwriter hopes to pitch her song to artists, producers and publishers. A song is an audio commodity. It must be heard for it to be appreciated. The demo is really the songwriter's business card.

For many beginning (or even experienced) songwriters, the challenge of creating a demo is a daunting one. Where do you start? When is a demo recording adequate? How much do you have to spend in order to create one that will catch the ear of recording artists or music industry professionals?

It's at this point in the writing process that songwriters become vulnerable to a myriad of experts whose suggestions range from one extreme to the other. Some say that as long as the song is strong, a simple guitar/vocal or piano/vocal suffices—that an artist, publisher or producer will be able to imagine what the song will sound like when it is fully produced. Others will tell you that because of the highly competitive nature of the music industry, your demo must be fully produced and radio-ready in order to receive a fair hearing.

As with most things in life—a balance between the two extremes is usually best. On one hand, every aspiring songwriter must face the hard, cold fact that her hobby (passion, obsession-compulsion) will cost money just like any other interest or pastime. On the other hand, most beginning songwriters don't have a fat bankroll to invest in demo production—especially if they are prolific writers with many songs. This is where a little common sense and a lot of creativity (something songwriters have in abundance anyway) can bridge the gap between extremes.

> *It is possible to create well-produced, professional demos that communicate your songs clearly and gain a hearing for you with local or national music professionals without having to put a second mortgage on your house or sell your firstborn.*

OK. Now I have a question for you. Do you know the most important question to ask yourself as you prepare to do a demo?

Is The Song Really Finished?

Exactly right! You must be sure to examine every note and every word to be absolutely certain it is exactly the way you want it. Personally, I like to make very rough demos of my new songs—a box tape recorder and the piano will do—so I can listen to them repeatedly in the car, in my headset as I jog, etc. It seems strange to say, but I find I have to learn my own song! As I become intimately familiar with it, I begin to hear places where it might be changed and improved—words or chords that can be re-worked to strengthen the over-all effect. Every time I listen to the rough demo, I pretend that I am a radio listener hearing the song for the very first time. I ask myself questions like:

♪ *Is the hook/title memorable and singable?*

♪ *Do the verses lead into and arrive at the chorus?*

♪ *Does the musical introduction create interest from the first note?*

♪ *What is the length of the song? Does it fall into that crucial 3 1/2 minute time frame so necessary for radio play?*

♪ *If I were a listener hearing this song for the first time, would I stay tuned or would I change the channel?*

The Chain Link Fence Phase

I often call this stage of the process the *Chain Link Fence Phase* of songwriting. If you've ever watched workmen putting up a chain link fence, you will understand the analogy. The first step is to put up the poles. Then the chain link is attached to the poles around the perimeter. When it is first attached, it sags and droops and looks pretty weak. But then the workers begin ratcheting the chain link with a come-along. With each ratcheting motion, the chain link gets tighter and tighter until you're sure they can't make it any tighter—and then they tighten it still more. When the fence is finished, a grown man can mount the chain link and it won't droop or sag at all! It has been drawn so tight that it is as strong as any other well-made chain link fence in the world.

That is our goal as songwriters—to tweak and ratchet every word and note until our song is as strong as or even stronger than any other song in its genre. As a friend of mine in the music industry wisely says: "If you're a songwriter trying to break into the music business from the outside, your songs don't have to be good...they have to be *bulletproof*."

The Importance of Feedback

At this point it may be worth your while to pull in another listening ear, someone objective who can hear past the roughness of the demo. (Probably not your mom or grandma who will love anything you do.)

Where Can I Find Such Objective Listeners?

Your Local Songwriters' Association

I can't say enough about the advantages of joining up! Songwriters' organizations are made up of people just like you who love to write songs—and the best part is that they live nearby. Most such organizations meet once or twice a month and host occasional seminars and workshops on the craft and business of music. Members range from complete beginners to semi-professional and sometimes professional writers.

Typically a part of each meeting is devoted to critiquing songs or songs-in-progress. You will find for the most part, that songwriters are darned honest people. They will give you some excellent feedback to consider.

Visit our website at **www.FromNowhereWithNothing.com** *for a current listing of local songwriters' associations in various parts of the country and around the world.*

In addition to having other songwriters listen to your work, it is helpful to have ordinary non-musical people give you their feedback.

> *Remember: It is non-musical listeners that make up the majority of those purchasing CDs and recorded products. It's not enough to impress other songwriters with your clever tunesmithing, you must also hook the average radio listener if you want to sell a million copies of your song.*

You will be amazed at the genius suggestions you'll receive from ordinary, not-especially-musical people who may think of something you haven't—something that could turn your song into a worldwide hit!

One songwriter who corresponds with me from Michigan was so desperate for objective feedback on her songs that she took her rough demo out to the local mall along with a stack of evaluation forms. She stopped a hundred people, asked them to listen to her song and then fill out a form answering questions similar to those listed above. She understood the importance of being absolutely sure a song is ready before proceeding with what can be the most expensive stage—the production of the professional demo.

A Professional Critique

There are many professional, published songwriters who will critique your song for a nominal fee. Professional songwriters can often see and hear things in your song that other less experienced listeners miss. They may also have suggestions about where you can pitch your song after it is demoed.

For a listing of recommended critiquing services refer to the resource pages at **www.FromNowhereWithNothing.com**.

Let me hasten to add that I understand your feeling a little defensive about letting other people evaluate your songs. We songwriters can be very emotionally attached to our creations. Our self-image is often at stake in the response of others to our work. We become ultra-sensitive to criticism—no matter how constructive and well intentioned it is. Critical remarks can seem like a personal attack. The only cure for this emotional attachment is to develop a thick skin and realize that great songs are not merely written—*they're re-written!* Remember, you don't have to make every change that is suggested, but if there are things that can be improved with a good edit or re-write, *now* is definitely the time to make those changes, before you invest money in the demo recording.

I can't tell you how sad it makes me to receive a demo from a songwriter who has obviously put a lot of money into the production of a wonderful recording, when it is obvious the song wasn't finished when the demo was made. No matter how great the production may be, it cannot conceal a poor or underdeveloped song. As a publisher and consultant, I am always reluctant to offer suggestions when I hear such recordings, because I know my critique will mean further expense for the writer who must then return to the studio to make the necessary changes.

> *Remember: Your Number One Goal as a song-writer is to make sure your songs communicate to the hearts of average people who hear them for the first time. Anything you can do to strengthen your song so that it really connects with listeners is much more easily done "before the fact," before the demo is produced.*

What Type Of Demo Does My Song Need?

A simple, straightforward ballad is often shown to best advantage in a high fidelity vocal recording with piano or guitar accompaniment. Blues and folk songs may require little more than a well-played guitar and a plaintive voice. A more uptempo number may need percussion, background vocals and a fuller production for it to shine. Common sense can guide you here. Remember: the word *demo* is short for *demonstration*. Your recording must adequately demonstrate the song you have written so that it connects with your listener and makes an emotional impact.

What Are My Recording Options?

DIY Technology

Until recently it was almost mandatory that you book a commercial studio to record a professional sounding demo. Commercial studios are usually quite expensive to book by the hour ($50-$100 or more) and often require a long wait between sessions owing to the high volume of clients. Thankfully, we now have many other options due largely to the proliferation of high-tech home studio systems and music software. You might be surprised just how many major label recordings are done in artists' homes and garage studios. As for production quality, it is often impossible to distinguish between CDs produced in commercial studios and those done at home. This is an unprecedented development and one that clearly favors DIYers and independents.

If you are a prolific writer with a good musical ear and some sequencing and engineering skills, you may want to consider purchasing your own equipment so that you are able to do as many demos as you wish without incurring studio costs. There are many affordable options these days—from simple four-track porta-studio systems to more sophisticated digital home studios. You can add as many bells and whistles as you like. With the wide range of keyboards available featuring sampled instrumental sounds it is possible to have a virtual orchestra at your disposal right in your own living room. Once you have sequenced the basic track, you may choose to overdub live instruments for a more acoustic live feel.

Caution: Do not record your demo tracks on keyboards with cheesy pre-programmed rhythm and instrumental settings.

As a publisher I receive demos almost every week from writers who recorded their songs using the canned sounds and default rhythms of keyboards designed for non-musicians. They have "non-professional" written all over them. Substandard equipment will not enhance your song's potential or its likelihood of being heard.

If you choose to develop your own studio system, it is important to research before you purchase. Do some reading and take some seminars on the various aspects of recording. Ask lots of questions and learn the various features of each brand of equipment. Once you make your purchase, remember—there will be a learning curve. It will take some time and patience to learn how to use the new software/hardware you have acquired.

Take it slowly…expect that it will take a while to perfect your skills and decide before you even begin that you will enjoy the process of learning.

Don't let yourself be overwhelmed by the many features of newly acquired technology. Focus on those you will need and use most. Add new skills a little at a time.

For further help in purchasing and learning to use recording equipment and software, visit our resource pages at **www.FromNowhereWithNothing.com**

Options for the Technologically Challenged

Perhaps, like me, you are just a simple songwriter with limited technical skills. What then?

RESEARCH YOUR MUSIC COMMUNITY

Savvy songwriters know that the key to affordable demo production is researching your music community and its options.

Start hanging out where musicians hang out. Ask questions. Network with musicians who possess the skills you lack. Your community's songwriters' club or association is an invaluable source of inside information on the resources available.

At songwriter meetings and critique sessions you will hear demos of songs by other writers in your area. When you come across one that is outstanding in its production and clarity, ask the writer where she recorded it. If it was in a commercial studio, find out which one and follow up with a telephone inquiry. Ask for a rate sheet and a demo of their work. If the demo was recorded in someone's home studio, make note of that as well—and after the songwriters' meeting buy that guy a cup of coffee!

Eventually, you will get to know your music community—from the best music equipment suppliers to the best-kept-secret studios. Don't forget to check out community colleges. Many have commercial music and media departments that operate like beauty schools. Those who have had their hair styled in a beauty school will know what I mean—students perform services under the watchful eye of an instructor. Great savings and good results are the norm.

THE BEAUTY OF BARTER

Remember, barter is a wonderful thing! As you get to know people in your music community, you will find you can trade services. This is a great way to cut recording costs. You may offer to sing backup on the demo of another writer in exchange for being allowed to use his home recording equipment. Networking is profitable and fun! We musicians may be a little flaky, but we're a big kick to hang out with.

MUSIC BY MAIL

You may well object that you live way, way out of town—100 miles or more beyond the Boondocks city limits. What if there are no studios, songwriting associations or music equipment stores nearby? Fear not—there remain options open to you. Many reputable producers will create a professional quality demo from your rough tape and a couple of phone conversations. Magazines such as *American Songwriter* contain dozens of classified ads from studios and musicians across the country—but especially in Nashville—who specialize in demo production.

In chapter one we examined some shark warnings and made a few recommendations to lyric writers seeking musicians to compose melodies. These apply to demo production as well. Be sure to review our tips if you are considering a long distance production.

Are My Expectations Realistic?

Writing a song is a truly euphoric experience. Songwriters often get so excited about their new songs they let their excitement carry them prematurely into the demo phase. You may feel a sudden urge to produce your own demo and even sing the lead vocal, but before you venture out, try to evaluate your skills objectively.

If you are relatively new at creating demos, you may want to rely on other, more experienced people to help you—especially at first.

Rely on Help From Others with More Experience

If you are new to songwriting and demo production, seek help from those with the experience you lack. As you network with songwriters and artists in your music community you will meet talented musicians, many of them experts in music production and audio technology. They can often be hired for a fixed fee (work-for-hire) to help produce your demo. Rarely, if ever, will they expect a percentage of copyright ownership.

There are several skills that are essential in creating an effective demo. You may well meet someone who possesses all the skills you require. It's good to be familiar with the following terms and their definitions:

♪ ***Sequencer***—*A musician who creates multi-track accompaniment recordings for your songs—from very simple productions to symphonic scores—using synthesized instruments and music software.*

♪ ***Arranger***—*Music arrangement is closely related to sequencing. A creative arrangement is crucial for capturing the potential of your song. As we noted in the first chapter, the fundamental elements of the song (words and melody) can be arranged in a number of harmonies and rhythms to suit a variety of tastes. A talented arranger/sequencer can help you brainstorm, using her creativity and knowledge of music theory to present your song in its best light.*

♪ ***Producer***—*The producer is responsible for the overall production of the recording—booking the studio, scheduling the singer(s) and live instrument players, negotiating fees etc.*

♪ ***Engineer***—*This is the person who operates all the knobs and sliders on the soundboard. When you book a commercial studio by the hour, an engi-*

neer is often provided at no additional charge. Experienced engineers usually have keen ears and may participate in the production and sequencing of the demo as well.

You may be lucky enough to find one talented individual who possesses all the above skills. Then again, you may have to coordinate the services of several people to get the job done. Keep your interactions with all involved in the demo production upbeat and work for good chemistry. Don't be intimidated into silence. Remain open to suggestions, but be sure to voice your opinions and preferences. This is your song. You are also, by the way, the one paying the bill!

Face Reality About the Vocals

If you have an adequate voice, you may want to sing the song yourself. You don't have to be the world's greatest singer in order to do a good demo. You must be able to sing on pitch, however, and have a voice that does not distract from the song's impact. In other words, if you are an operatic tenor and you have just written a down-and-dirty Blues song, you may not be the right singer for the demo. Face it, get over it, and find someone who can sing the Blues like Blues are supposed to be sung!

What Else Is Important For Great Vocals?

Locate the Best Demo Singers in Your Area

Network…network…network! Visit local clubs and attend performances. Sit in on the recording sessions of other songwriters. Meet vocal coaches in your town and ask them about their students. Inquire in church and college music departments. Be especially alert for singers who have also had recording experience. An experienced vocalist can be an invaluable ingredient in creating a demo you will be proud of.

Practice Before You Get to the Studio

Contact your demo singer well in advance to get acquainted and talk about the song. Provide the singer with a rough work tape of the song and find out which key she prefers. Insist on a practice session before you go into the studio. Once inside the studio the meter will be running. You don't want to use expensive studio time to teach the singer the song.

Don't Make the Listener Strain to Hear the Lyrics

It is extremely important that your song's lyrics are clearly enunciated and that when the recording is mixed, the vocals are upfront and not buried in the instrumental tracks. Sometimes musicians get so caught up in the intricacies of the demo's instrumental components that they seem to add the vocals almost as an afterthought.

Clearly articulated lyrics are crucial, *especially if you mean to have your song recorded by a major artist.* When words can't be made out, publishers quickly lose interest in a song and consign it to the nearest circular file.

> *Remember: The essential ingredients of your song are its words and melody. Since both are conveyed by the vocals, it is imperative they be articulated clearly.*

Be Receptive to Vocal Suggestions but Stick to Your Guns

Be open to the singer's inspiration, but don't be afraid to require her to record the song in a manner you think fit. Watch phrasing especially, so that rhymes are captured and the music is effectively communicated.

Use Background Vocals Tastefully

Background vocals can add a great deal to the overall feel of a song, but don't be pressured into doing a full complement of background vocals unless the song requires it. Sometimes less is more in this department.

What's The Most Important Feature of The Demo?

The most important feature of any demo recording is that the song be clear and easily appreciated. If your demo is fuzzy and the words are hard to hear, you will give the impression that you are an amateur and the force of your lyrics and melody will be lost. Most publishers and music executives will not listen for more than a few seconds before turning off a poorly recorded demo.

CD vs. Cassette

It is precisely because clarity is so important that CDs have become the exclusive medium for professional demos. The CD is much truer to the master recording than the cassette with its hiss and background noise. Also, when copies are made of copies, cassettes become progressively less clear and more distorted.

Rarely, if ever, are cassettes used for pitching demos to music professionals these days, so decide in advance that you will only produce and pitch CD demos, unless the publisher or music professional specifically requests a cassette. Although CD duplication may be a bit more expensive at first (purchasing a CD burner and the correct software), CDs are now much less expensive per unit than cassettes when purchased in bulk, and since they are lightweight, they are also less expensive to mail.

Yikes...Anything Else?

I know we have covered a lot of ground here, but remember:

> *Your demo is your audio calling card and one of the costlier aspects of songwriting. Meticulous care on the front end means less expense overall and a demo that makes the right impression.*

As your demo is nearing completion, your excitement is sure to build. It's always so rewarding to hear with your ears what you have only imagined for so long. There are several things to consider, however, before you finish recording and mixing.

Listen to the Final Mix in Your Car with the Motor Running

Does this sound flaky? It's no joke. Most recorded music is listened to in the car either on the radio or on a CD player. The car engine will be running; there will be ambient street noise, and who knows how much clamor from children fighting in the back seat? This is the real world of the average music listener. If it doesn't sound good here, you may want to make some changes to the final mix. Don't use the pristine setting of the studio as the plumb line to measure the clarity and mix of your demo.

Ask for at Least Two Full Mix Masters of Your Demo

When your demo is finished, ask for at least two master copies of your song on CD. Keep one of them unused in your file as a backup. Use the other to make copies for pitching purposes. This way you will never mess up your one-and-only master copy.

Consider Doing a Male and a Female Lead Vocal

If your song is appropriate for either a male or female singer, it may be wise to cut one version of each—even if that involves a little more upfront expense in the studio. Later, when you begin pitching your song to artists, you will have a male version of the song for male artists, and a female version for female artists.

You might think that the gender of the demo singer would not matter all that much. Surely an artist will hear the song's possibilities in either gender, right? Don't bank on it! When artists are listening to hundreds of demos with a view to selecting just ten or twelve to record, gender may play a bigger role in deciding the suitability of your song than you might first be inclined to think. If your demo singer's gender does not match that of the artist considering your song, the discrepancy may create just enough of a negative to predispose the artist against it.

Be Sure You Request Tracks Only—Preferably in Two Keys

It is a small matter for the engineer to give you a track mix of your song without the lead vocal. Ask for one. This may come in handy should you or another singer wish to perform your song. The track mix is also useful should you decide to change some of the lyrics at a later date. If you already have a track mix, it is much less expensive and far more convenient to re-record a new vocal after changes to the lyrics have been made.

If you are doing two versions of the tracks anyway (for a male and a female singer) you will probably have to change keys to accommodate your vocalists. It is a good idea to have accompaniment tracks in at least two keys—one in a higher key for soprano and tenor voices, another in a medium-low key for alto or baritone voices.

If your tracks are sequenced with software using synthesized sounds, it is usually a snap to adjust the key and cut another track. If you have overdubbed live instruments, you may need to ask your live players to add their parts in both keys. Often this can be done in one take and involves a minimum of effort and expense.

Here's why it's smart to have tracks in two keys:

♫ You may pitch your song to a regional or national artist who is interested in recording it for an upcoming project. If you already have accompaniment tracks in her key, it will assist her as she practices and learns the song.

♫ You may decide to *lease* your tracks to artists for recording purposes. You will find many independent artists with little or no studio experience who are keen to produce inexpensive recordings as a way to learn the ropes. Or they may need CD demos featuring their own voices to include with promotional material. These artists are often grateful to pay for the use of completed tracks because they help keep studio costs low. Leasing tracks is also a good way of recouping expenses you have incurred—a win-win situation. The lease fee is totally negotiable and may be determined in part by how elaborately produced the track is.

Watch for Sales on Bulk Blank CDs

The price of blank CDs keeps going down. If you shop carefully in computer or office supply houses, you can find sales on 100 unit spindles of good quality blank CDs. Become familiar with prices…compare…use coupons and rebates. I have been able to purchase blank CDs during sales for as little as five cents a piece!

A Final Word Of Advice

No matter how experienced you are as a writer, no matter how many demos you have done, you will always be able to find fault with your work. Be critical, but unless you have made some glaring error, you do well to simply learn from the mistakes of a less-than-perfect recording session and move on to the next song. Nearly everyone's early demos are poorer in quality than those they produce after years of practice.

Even if your recording doesn't turn out exactly as you had hoped, don't hesitate to pitch your slightly imperfect demo to local artists looking for material. If they pick your song to record, they will probably do a new (and perhaps better) arrangement and production of it. It's more important to be pitching your songs than waiting to create the perfect demo. Do the very best you can and keep striving to do better the next time.

I remember judging a song competition several years ago. After listening to hundreds of songs, the other judge and I felt as though we were bleeding at the ears. Then, out of the pile came a beautiful mellow melody joined to some lovely words. The song was called *Fields of Grace*. It was a very simple ballad—just an electric piano and voice. There were even a couple bloopers in the piano track. And yet, the song was unmistakably wonderful! It made me want to meet the writer. This experience reinforced an important principle for me: As important as the demo is, the song is everything!

If you have written a killer song, I can guarantee that it will be hard to ruin it with your demo, no matter how much of a novice you are at production. Think about The Beatles' early recordings in the 1960s. Technology and sound recording were much more primitive than they are today. In production terms, those early albums sound pretty rough. And yet, those same recordings are still topping the charts today. Why? Because The Beatles wrote great songs!

Have fun doing your demo! This gig is about progress—not perfection!

REWIND...

~ Be sure your song is really finished. It needs to be as tight and strong as a chain link fence before you invest in producing a demo to pitch.

~ Research all your recording options. Look at DIY technology and all other affordable production resources.

~ Have realistic expectations and learn as you grow. Enjoy the process.

NOTES

4

The Presentation

At last! Your demo is finished, and you can't quit listening to it. There is nothing quite like finally hearing with your own ears what you have only played in your head. You are sure this song will be the next blockbuster hit—if only you can get it into the hands of that artist who can take it to the top of the charts. What do you do next?

You'll need to create a package that will put your song in the best possible light. Before your demo finds its way to a music professional's CD player, it must first pass before her eyes.

So How Important Is The Presentation Anyway?

You might think the visual appearance of your CD is not all that important. It's all about the song, right? Well, yes…and no.

Think about it this way: Curvaceous Cathy is applying for a job as a swimsuit model. She has a drop-dead figure and a gorgeous face. But the day she applies for the job, she dons an ill-fitting dress, skips the makeup and pulls her hair back into a half-combed ponytail. What are the chances she'll be chosen for the next *Sports Illustrated Swimsuit Issue*? You tell me.

You may be a mystery writer with a killer plot that is so intriguing it is destined for the Best Seller List. You take months writing and re-writing the story until it is absolutely perfect. The editor of a major publishing house agrees to see you. But when you show up for your appointment, you hand her your masterpiece in a spiral notebook, scrawled in No. 2 pencil. Is she likely to form a favorable impression of your story—that is, if she even bothers to read it? If you think so, I have a great piece of oceanfront property in South Dakota I would like to sell you.

As a music publisher, I never cease to be amazed at the way songs are packaged and posted to me. Recordings are frequently of very poor quality; lyrics are either not included or handwritten, often illegibly. In many cases it is difficult to locate the writer's name, address and phone number. I sometimes wonder why someone would go to the effort and expense to produce a professional demo but give so little thought to an attractive visual presentation of the posted product. I realize the song is the main feature. The fact remains that the recipient is going to see the package before she ever hears the song. It is therefore essential that you approach the presentation of your demo as thoughtfully and as tastefully as you approached the recording of it.

> *Even with very limited funds, a clean and professional package is a must if you hope to win a hearing for your song.*

Do I Have To Have A Slick Package For Every Demo I Give Out?

The way you present your song lets the recipient know how you feel about your work. Your careful attention to this small but important matter leaves an impression. It says "self-assurance" and "professionalism." When you package your song attractively, it enhances your credibility as a songwriter.

You will be pitching your song to many different kinds of people. As you get to know your local music community, you'll discover independent artists who are looking for original songs like yours. You may have an opportunity to meet a major artist who is coming through town for an in-store appearance at a record retailer. You'll present your songs to music industry producers and publishers if you visit a major music city and you'll probably be asked to mail a copy of your demo after an initial phone or email contact. Wherever your song goes and whoever's on the receiving end, a great demo in a clean package will let people know you mean to be taken seriously.

So...What Do I Need For A Professional Presentation?

Business Stationery

If you intend to pursue songwriting as more than a hobby, an attractive letterhead, business envelopes, shipping labels, CD labels and business cards are professional necessities. But this need not be an expensive proposal. The advantage of desktop publishing technology is that you or a friend may design a smart letterhead at little or no cost. Printing fees vary considerably. With the right computer software and a little learning curve time, you may be able to print your own stationery at home. But be sure you don't sacrifice a professional image just to save a buck.

If you don't have the skills to do high quality printing at home, shop around until you find a printer you can afford. The office supply superstores (Office Depot, Office Max, Staples, etc.) have copy centers that can print small quantities of stationery at affordable prices. Choose classy paper. Peruse the full range of styles in a panorama of colors and textures.

Creative Identification

You may decide to name your songwriting enterprise, and make the company name the focus of your artwork. You may even choose to design a simple logo.

Some time ago I received a sharp looking package from a songwriter whose last name was Carr. He had named his songwriting business Carr Tunes. That was clever and made his package stand out. I continued to receive material from him, and came in time to associate his name and letterhead with songs that are elegantly created and presented.

Points to remember:

♪ *Make sure your letterhead clearly displays your name, postal address, phone and fax numbers, email address and website.*

♪ *For each song in your submission package, include a typed lyric sheet on your letterhead. That way your identifying information is never separated from your lyrics.*

♪ *Be sure your contact information—telephone numbers, physical and email addresses—is printed on your CD labels. Right-brained music execs are notorious for losing things! Do everything you can to ensure that if they listen to and like your song, they won't have to search to find you, the writer.*

♪ *Choose a clear and legible font. Some fonts—especially those in script—may be very artistic, but quite difficult to read. The objective here is not to be artsy, but to make your lyric sheet as legible as possible. If a lyric sheet is difficult to read and follow, your listener may become distracted. And this can mean the difference between a cut on a recording and a rejection letter.*

♪ *Bold and center the title of your song on the page. Then type the first verse. When you reach the chorus, label it "Chorus." Indent to set it apart. Then proceed with the second verse. If the song has a bridge, label it "Bridge" and again, indent. This makes it easy for a busy music executive or recording artist to review the song at a glance without searching to identify its parts.*

♪ *Block out your lyrics as you would a poem and be sure to show off your rhyme patterns. Many songwriters write their lyrics in paragraph style, so it's not clear if there is a rhyme scheme at all. As my husband says, "It's a pretty poor dog that won't wag his own tail!" You worked hard to create these lyrics—put your creative talent on display.*

♪ *Finally, at the bottom of the page, type the name(s) of the writer(s) of the song. Below the names type: Copyright 2007/Your Name—or if your word processor has the copyright symbol— ©—you can simply type: ©Year/Your Name. This is really the only copyright you will need for the time being.*

As you'll remember from our discussion in chapter two, a song is automatically protected under the present copyright law from the moment it is fixed on paper or in a recording (no matter how rough). Be sure the copyright notice is clearly featured on your lyric sheet as well as on your CD label.

Information on registering your copyright with the US Copyright Office is covered in Appendix A. See Appendix B for examples of both poorly-written and well-written lyric sheets.

Do I Need A Lead Sheet?

Many songwriters mistakenly believe that publishers and record companies expect a lead sheet or other sheet music to be part of the presentation packet. (For beginners who may not be familiar with the term, a lead sheet is simply the melody line written on music paper with chord changes notated above the melody.) The truth is that in most cases music professionals prefer that you not include written music at all. A lyric sheet and demo CD are quite sufficient. If and when they decide to publish or record your song, they will have their own arrangers and musicians do the score.

How Many Songs Should I Submit At Once?

It is usually a good idea to limit the number of demos in any one submission packet to two or three. From time to time you may find it necessary to submit as many as five or six songs—or even more. This is often the case when you are pitching material to local artists or producers for an upcoming project. They may ask to hear songs from your catalog in a variety of styles to aid in the selection process.

If you are submitting several lyric sheets at once, the important thing to remember is to keep the package neat. I have often used clear plastic report folders with slide spines to hold the lyric sheets and cover letter together. The CD demo may then be slipped inside the folder so that all portions of your submission can be removed from the envelope in one motion.

Some music professionals prefer to have the lyric sheet folded around the CD case and attached with a rubber band to keep them together. This is an especially good idea if you are submitting songs for a songwriting contest. Make sure that everything is marked with your contact information so that neither you nor your song falls between the cracks.

What About Labeling The CDs Themselves?

It is a good idea to purchase CD labeling software that allows you to print the title(s) of your song(s) and contact information on a CD label with your word processor. You may select a printer that writes directly on the surface of a printable CD. Whatever you decide, don't handwrite anything! It reeks of amateurism and no matter how neat your handwriting is, it will not show your song to its best advantage.

What Kind Of CD Case Is Best?

There are all kinds of CD cases—from hard plastic to flexible poly to simple paper sleeves. Consider two things:

Protection of the Demo

It simply won't do to have your CD damaged en route. If you have included lyric sheets in your packet, you may be able to slip the CD between the sheets to pad and protect it. Be sure to use padded envelopes for mailing. If you choose a paper CD sleeve, you may want to protect it by placing it between two thin pieces of cardboard. If you decide on a plastic case, look for a thin, lightweight one. Whatever you choose, take care to ensure that your CD arrives safely.

I learned this lesson the hard way. In a rush to post a demo for consideration by a major label artist I used a paper CD sleeve and failed to sufficiently protect the CD with added padding. As a result the demo arrived cracked and I forfeited my chance at a big cut. I won't make that mistake again.

Mailing Costs

The case you choose can greatly influence the cost of postage. If you plan to do a lot of pitching by mail, opting for a lightweight case can mean substantial savings.

Should I Include A Cover Letter?

A brief cover letter is appropriate…but the key word here is *brief*.

Music professionals do not want an exhaustive musical resume or a synopsis of how the enclosed song was inspired. Nor will they want to see photocopies of articles about you. A simple and polite introduction together with a short description of the song—title, genre and tempo—will suffice. If the song you are sending is intended for a specific artist, be sure to mention her name.

Specific tips for writing the cover letter are provided in Appendix B together with a sample to guide you as you draft your own.

What If I Also Want To Pitch Myself As An Artist?

If you are an artist as well as a songwriter, you may wish to pitch yourself, as well as your songs, for performance gigs and a recording contract. In this case your package will be more like a promotional kit. It should include a photo of yourself, a brief bio and a few well-chosen endorsements from people who have heard your music.

The Folder

Promo packets come in all shapes and sizes. Costs vary widely. With some imagination and planning, you can create a very impressive promo package without breaking the bank. The key, I believe, is planning. Shop around for a nice looking folder—don't go for the least expensive one. First impressions are critical.

Remember: You are too poor and unknown to be cheap!

The Photograph

Have a good photograph made of you! There are a number of companies that create photographs for promotional purposes. Some of these are OK, but most are variations of the same head shot—*Boring*!

Several months ago we received a beautiful promo packet from an aspiring singer-songwriter who is also a guitarist. The folder was glossy black with the artist's name printed on the front. When you opened it, instead of the usual tedious headshot, there was a photo of the artist walking toward the camera along some railroad tracks with his guitar over his shoulder.

A simple variation, but one so striking it instantly sparked our interest! The folder featured a built-in CD case. When you removed the CD demo, another photo of the artist was revealed—only this time from the rear as he walked away from the camera along the same railroad tracks. Creative! Impressive! Before we had even heard the CD, our estimation of the artist had gone up a dozen notches.

Background Material

Be very choosy about the printed material you include in your promo packet.

The goal is not to give music professionals your complete life story. The trick is to excite their interest so that they will contact you. Nine times out of ten, less is more.

Keep your promo packet simple and clean. Avoid including lengthy newspaper articles about your accomplishments and your music—no matter how flattering they may be. Music execs have neither time nor inclination to wade through all that. Create an *Endorsements Page* containing short excerpts from several significant sources with raves about your music. Do not include a business resume with all of your credits since junior high. They will not be interested! If they like what they hear and see, you can fill them in on your personal history later. Brevity is the name of the game with your promo packet!

Example of an Outstanding Promo Packet

On several occasions I have been invited to serve as a judge for Master Vocal Showcases hosted by Septien Vocal Productions here in Dallas. Linda Septien has had a long and successful career as a vocal teacher and coach and has been instrumental in launching the careers of nationally recognized artists such as Jessica Simpson, Ashlee Simpson and Ryan Cabrera. She also coached the sensational girl band, Destiny's Child. Linda's showcases are always first-class productions, with press kits on each performing vocalist at the judges' stations.

The press kits, designed by Linda and her graphics team, are sturdy, laminated one-sheets with creative photos of the artist on each side. The printed information is extremely brief, focusing on unique aspects of the artist's music. It includes a couple of short endorsements from well-known music industry professionals. On the back is a CD pocket containing the artist's demo.

I can't tell you how impressed I was by these visually inviting, yet concise promotional tools. They are easy to pop into a brief case; they are self-contained and almost indestructible; their slick, hip appearance made me sit up and take notice of these young artists. Most importantly, it made me want to hear their CDs. The key to the effectiveness of these promos is their photography and layout. Care is taken to ensure that visuals are representative of the artist's age and style. To view a sample you may visit Linda's website at **www.TheSeptienGroup.com**.

What About EPKs And MP3s?

Just a word about electronic press kits (EPKs) and pitching songs over the Internet as audio files. The Internet has of course opened new avenues for the transmission of data that can be very expedient in the time-sensitive world of music. Nowadays, there are many web-based companies that can be retained to create extremely impressive electronic promotional material. Keep in mind that…

> *Unless you have made personal contact with a music professional who has explicitly requested an electronic presentation, it is best to send your material by mail.*

Audio files and music promos require a lot of disk space to download. It is more than a little presumptuous to impose your music on a busy professional by sending her a huge unsolicited file. I am always a little annoyed when unknown writers approach me in this manner. I much prefer to receive material by mail so that I can review it at my convenience.

TO SUMMARIZE

The presentation package is like the frame of a painting. You wouldn't ordinarily hang a paint-by-numbers picture in an elegant frame. But when you have studied art, perfected your skills and created a masterpiece, an elegant frame becomes indispensable. The frame is not the most important thing—the painting is what people will remember. Still the frame has the power to significantly enhance or diminish the painting's impact.

Your package reflects how you feel about your songs and yourself as a writer. The presumption is that if you have put a lot of effort into your craft, it will be evident in the presentation. If you have worked hard to become a song craftsman, and if you are writing hit material, you will display it carefully and attractively. Take time to develop your package. It contains your masterpiece!

Rewind....

Your carefully produced demo must pass a visual test before it is heard.

The keys to effective presentation are:

1) Careful Planning

2) Creativity

3) Neatness

4) Brevity

NOTES

5

Deal or No Deal?

A QUICK REVIEW

So...there you are, still in Boondocks, Montana! But—if you've been follow-ing our suggestions—you've taken some pretty good strides down the road to success. You've been playing one of the two main roles of a music publish-er by mentoring yourself. You've developed a disciplined reading program and kept up with your songwriting exercises. You've experienced the demo production process and have good, clear demos of your carefully crafted songs. You've created an attractive presentation packet that displays your songs in their best possible light.

Now What?

It is at this point that you need to don the other hat of the music publisher—the *promoter's hat*—and find ways to get your song(s) to the world. For many, this part of the process is the most intimidating because it involves the business of music—a business whose reputation makes it appear overwhelm-ingly complicated and larger-than-life. It is at this point that even gifted song-writers give up their dreams because they simply have no idea how or where to get started or what they need to know.

This is a watershed moment!

Option 1: You may wish to avoid acquiring a basic knowledge of music as an industry, and continue to write songs as a hobbyist, for your own pleasure and that of your family and friends.

Option 2: If you want to pursue songwriting as a career, and make some money doing it, you will have to learn the essentials of songwriting as a business.

If you opt for 2, approach it as a creative challenge. You will find that it can be quite interesting and even fun—and I *guar-awn-tee* that you will receive an education in the process. You may learn things you never wanted to know, but you will evolve into a more savvy, wary and skilled professional than you ever dreamed you could be.

Before we even begin to talk about the business of songwriting, I want to make it very clear that this book in general—and this chapter in particular—do not exhaust the subject of music publishing. The information contained here is meant simply to acquaint you with its most basic terms and how they may apply to you as you begin "doing it yourself" from Boondocks.

There are many good books and articles that detail the intricate nuances of this complex subject in a thoroughgoing manner. I recommend a number of titles below. Bear in mind that an experienced entertainment attorney is an indispensable resource for any contractual agreements you may be considering.

So How And When Am I Going To "Sell" One Of My Songs?

This question frequently appears in my inbox. It usually indicates unfamiliarity with the way songs make money. Aspiring songwriters are keen to begin making a living on their talent. "Show me the money," they say. But they haven't the foggiest idea how songs generate revenue.

Songs are rarely sold outright if the songwriter has any business savvy. There is only one time a song is really sold—and that is under a *work-for-hire* agreement, but I'm not even going to tell you what that is until you acquire a basic grasp of how music business is conducted.

If you stay with me through this chapter, I'll tell you how you can "sell a song" at the end of it. Deal?

Deal! So What Do I Need To Know?

Probably the most important thing to know about the music business is that it is extremely fluid. Copyright law evolves so quickly that only the most experienced and dedicated attorneys, specializing in music and entertainment, are able to keep up with it.

> *At the bottom line, every negotiation is a crapshoot. You're gambling that what you have written is worth what you say it's worth. It's a poker hand. You have to know when to hold and when to fold. When it's a deal...or no deal.*

Attorneys and advisors can help you see the issues in a negotiation, but you are the decision maker in the end. Unless you understand the basics of the business, you won't understand what your advisors are telling you. So let's familiarize ourselves with some fundamentals.

Copyright

We touched on the word *copyright* in chapter two. As you will recall, in addition to the right to copy, reproduce, publish and sell a song, the word is often used to refer to the song itself (as in "he is the owner of the copyright").

Intellectual Property

Copyrights are considered *intellectual property*. This phrase means any created product generated by human intellect that is unique, novel, unobvious and has some value in the marketplace. It can refer to an idea, an invention, a business method or a computer program—but for us songwriters, our intellectual property is our songs.

Intellectual property has many of the same attributes as other kinds of property. It is considered a personal asset and can therefore be bought, sold, licensed or willed to others. The owner has the right to prevent unauthorized use of intellectual property, just as she would have the right to prevent unauthorized trespassing on a piece of real estate. The one major difference between intellectual property and other assets is that it is intangible and cannot be identified by physical descriptions or boundaries. Intellectual property must be *expressed* in some way in order to be protected by copyright law.

Now, I understand that our songs are more like our children than inanimate property. We songwriters are very emotionally attached to these musical creations. That attachment is unlikely to change. (Just let anybody try to tell us that our baby is ugly.) But while we continue to love our songs as expressions of ourselves, we must also learn to look at them objectively as sources of revenue generation.

Royalty

The next term we need to understand is the word *royalty*. A royalty is an agreed portion of the income from a work paid to its author or composer. There are many kinds of royalties and new royalties pop up every day as advancing technology multiplies the ways that songs can be used for profit. Let's take a moment to define some of the most basic.

1. MECHANICAL ROYALTIES

Definition: Mechanical royalties are payments by a record company or an independent artist to a copyright owner (the songwriter or the songwriter's publisher if there is one) for the right to use a song in recordings.

Statutory Mechanical Rate

The statutory rate for mechanical royalties fluctuates. Fortunately for us songwriters, it usually goes up each time it changes. In years past, a five-person panel appointed by the President of the United States and confirmed by the Senate set the mechanical royalty rate. This panel—called the Copyright Royalty Tribunal (CRT)—determined the current statutory rate for mechanical licenses based on changes in the Consumer Price Index. In 1993, the Library of Congress assumed this responsibility using the same adjustment formula. The rate is usually raised 1/2 cent every other year. At the time of this writing the statutory rate for mechanical licenses stood at 9.1 cents per song for each manufactured unit.

In other words, when an artist who manufactures 1,000 CDs includes one of your songs on her recording, the mechanical royalties for that one song are $91. This amount is paid by the artist's record company or—if the artist is an independent—by the recording artist herself. It is payable to the songwriter's publisher (if there is one) or to the songwriter directly if there is no publisher involved. If there is a publisher, the songwriter and the publisher share this amount according to the songwriting agreement between them (usually a 50/50 split).

Reduced Rate

I bet I can read your mind right now! You're saying to yourself, "Heck, the songwriter sure ain't getting much out of this deal—a measly $91 on 1,000 records?" Well, you'll be even more amazed to learn that record labels and recording artists often request a 75 percent rate on mechanical royalty payments. Often they ask for even bigger reductions. And believe it or not, sometimes a reduced rate turns out to be a win-win situation for both the copyright owner and the record label.

If, for instance, a household-name artist on a major record label plans to manufacture a half million units of a new CD featuring your song, it may be in the song's (and your) best interest to allow the reduced rate. At 75 percent of the current statutory rate (9.1 cents) your song would earn $34,125, and the record label would save $11,375. Not too shabby for either party! It's much better to have 75 percent of something big than 100 percent of nothing.

Let's consider another scenario: you are one in a group of copyright owners pitching songs for an upcoming recording. The others agree to give the record label a reduced rate to increase the likelihood their songs will be selected. In this case you may wisely choose to join them. Only, be sure your contract contains a *Most Favored Nations Clause* (or…in Boondocks vernacular…an *I Wanna Get What Everyone Else is Getting Clause*). It states that should the other writers start receiving a higher rate, you will too.

If, however, you are dealing with an independent artist manufacturing a one-time order of 1000 CDs, note that the 75 percent rate lowers the $91 due you for the use of your song to just $68.25 (which, you will recall, must be shared with any co-writers or publishers who have a stake in the ownership of the copyright).

Before you get caught up in the excitement of having one of your songs recorded, get out your calculator…do a little simple math…then decide.

First Use

The law permits the owner of the copyright to authorize which artist will use a song first. This is called the *first use*. The artist or company that wishes to use a never-before-recorded song must request a mechanical licensing agreement from the copyright owner who has the right to decide whether or not to issue the agreement and at what price (courtesy usually dictates that the royalties follow the statutory rate). The recording must be distributed for sale to the public in order to qualify as a first use. After this, however, the law states that any artist can cover the song. Each user must contact the publisher for a licensing agreement and must pay mechanical royalties.

2. PERFORMANCE ROYALTIES

Definition: Performance royalties differ from mechanical royalties in that they are not based on the number of units of music product manufactured, but on the number of performances the song receives over the radio, on television, Muzak systems, at ticketed concerts, through Internet music streaming, etc. Performance royalties in the United States are paid directly to the songwriter or to each of the songwriters (in a co-write) and to the music publisher through one of the three Performing Rights Organizations (PROs)—ASCAP, BMI or SESAC.

Performing Rights Organizations

PROs receive monies by issuing blanket licenses to radio and TV stations and networks, as well as to clubs, restaurants and other performance sites. Then they monitor the number of performances of the titles in their catalogs and pay their songwriter and publisher members for the right to perform their copyrighted works. They are, in a way, collecting "rent" on intellectual property and paying the owners.

Many beginning songwriters mistakenly believe that when they have joined one of these organizations, their songs have been published. This is incorrect and leads to much confusion. Performing rights organizations survey songs performed through licensees and pay the writers (and/or publishers) based on the number of plays a given song receives within a royalty period.

Every songwriter whose songs are receiving airplay or being performed in ticketed venues should belong to one of the three PROs. She ought to be sure that each original song is properly registered with the organization. As a writer you are only allowed to belong to one PRO at a time.

Each performing rights organization has different strengths and unique features. It is up to the songwriter to research her options and choose the PRO that best suits her needs. A good way to start is by paying a visit to each PRO website. Take some time—or make several web visits—to carefully peruse the features and services offered. If you have specific questions, don't hesitate to call the organization and ask to speak to a Member Services Representative, who will be able to interact with you personally and facilitate the registration process when you are ready to join. The web addresses are:

ASCAP **www.ascap.com**
BMI   **www.bmi.com**
SESAC **www.sesac.com**

3. Synchronization Royalties

Definition: These are royalties paid for the use of songs that are synchronized to accompany a movie or video.

Songwriting Opportunities in Film

Today more and more films are being produced independently on limited budgets, allowing unknown songwriters to pitch their original songs for use in films. Film producers will often try to get the songwriter to allow the use of a song at little or no cost.

You may be very wise to consider such a proposal simply for the exposure and credibility it will give you as a writer. It is, however, imperative that you weigh this decision carefully. There have been many who "sold out cheap" for the sake of exposure and then saw their songs become the identifying themes for films or television shows that might have supplied them a lifetime revenue stream had they negotiated differently. This is just one instance when you need an experienced entertainment lawyer to advise you before you grab the pen and sign on the dotted line.

Wow! Are There Other Kinds Of Royalties?

We're really only scratching the surface here. There are almost as many kinds of royalties as there are ideas for how songs can be used. There are, of course, print royalties for the use of songs in sheet music, folios or collections. There are royalties for songs used as parodies, in advertising campaigns, on the Internet, in karaoke tracks and as ring tones for cell phones.

As a beginning songwriter in Boondocks, your primary concern will probably be the mechanical royalties you stand to earn by placing your songs on recordings by independent artists in your area. If you are fortunate enough to begin receiving radio play you may start to collect some performance royalties (although don't hold your breath on this one…performance royalties take a long time to kick in and don't amount to much until your song receives major airplay or is widely performed).

Now is the time to start educating yourself. Begin by reading books on the music business that are easy to understand. My favorites are:

> **Music Publishing: a Songwriter's Guide**
> by Randy Poe (Writers Digest)
> **All You Need to Know About the Music Business**
> by Donald S. Passman (Simon & Schuster)
> **This Business of Songwriting**
> by Jason Blume (Billboard Books)

Other helpful books on this important subject can be found on our resource pages at **www.FromNowhereWithNothing.com**.

Do I Have To Issue A Mechanical License Agreement If Someone Wants To Record My Song?

In order to collect mechanical royalties professionally, it will be necessary for you to issue the artist a mechanical license. Please don't freak out! It isn't all that hard to create a mechanical license that you can use for each artist who wishes to record your songs.

A wonderful resource is *The Musician's Business and Legal Guide,* a publication of the Beverly Hills Bar Association. It contains gobs of valuable and accurate information on many subjects related to the music industry. One of its most valuable assets, in my opinion, is a template for a simple mechanical license you can adapt and use as you issue your own agreements. The book can be ordered through the Beverly Hills Bar Association website at **www.bhba.org** or you may call: 310-601-BHBA. This book is a must-have. It is sure to save you lots of time and money. Stop reading right here and order it…I'll wait till you get back…

…Did you order it? Great. You have just taken an important step in developing a professional approach to your songwriting business. Remember that it's much better to start right than to try to dig yourself out of a hole later on.

As your song catalog grows, you may decide to take advantage of a licensing collection resource like the Harry Fox Agency. Harry Fox issues mechanical licenses on behalf of publishers for a commission fee that comes off the top of any income earned by songs it manages. The agency also helps to collect royalties due to publishers from deadbeat record companies that may use a song without following through financially. You can find out more about the Harry Fox Agency by visiting them online at **wwwHarryFox.com**. Whether to use an agency like Harry Fox or to issue your own licenses is a decision only you can make. Think and study carefully before you decide.

What If I'm Asked To Waive Mechanical Royalties In Exchange For The Exposure My Song Will Receive On A Record?

Remember that you—as the writer and the owner of the song—are the *de facto* publisher unless or until you enter into an agreement with another company. As you grow in your craft and network your local arts community, you will inevitably find singers who are looking for original material and want to record your songs. This is very exciting for you as the songwriter, but a word of caution here:

> *Don't let your excitement keep you from handling the business aspects of the recording in a professional way.*

Songwriters are often approached by independent artists who expect the writer to waive mechanical royalties in exchange for the "phenomenal exposure" a song is likely to receive on the artist's 1,000 manufactured CDs. My advice to you is that you resist this logic.

In my opinion it is wrong on two levels:

1. IT IS UNPROFESSIONAL

If you allow an artist to get by without paying what you are owed, it creates the impression that you do not take your music seriously. Your professionalism depends in large measure on your having and communicating a true estimate of your talents and the value of your work. Let's face it: if the artist didn't have songs to sing, she wouldn't have a CD at all. Your song is valuable intellectual property. It is an indispensable part of the project. The artist would never consider asking the engineer, the studio, the graphic designer or the manufacturer to waive their fees for the recording. Why should the songwriter be expected to?

2. It Creates Unhealthy Expectations

If you don't insist on payment, you are teaching new artists to expect this kind of bargain with other songwriters. It lowers the value of the songwriter's contribution in general and perpetuates the myth that your intellectual property is swampland rather than prime real estate.

If you and the artist are friends and collaborators, and if you really want to help the artist financially, my suggestion is that you give a cash gift to help defray expenses. But don't waive the royalties due you.

Caveat

The above suggestions are aimed at independent artist recordings only. If you have the good fortune to secure a cut on a major artist recording, you may be asked to include the artist as a co-writer on your song—even if she didn't write a word or a note of it. If you still own the copyright and are acting as your own publisher, you may also be required to give up all or part of the publisher's share in order to guarantee a place on the recording.

Of course, if the stakes are high enough and the opportunity for recognition is promising enough, it may be worth making some concessions in the interest of promoting your work. Only you can decide whether the trade off is worth it.

How Do I Know When To Consult A Lawyer About This Stuff?

Competent legal counsel is one of the first and most essential services a songwriter will require. All jokes about unscrupulous lawyers aside, I have found most are great allies when it comes to watching the songwriter's back. Lawyers understand all the facets of this crazy business. They think of ways to protect songs, increase income and enhance a writer's cache—things that often never occur to artists.

That said, it probably won't be necessary to run out and hire a lawyer as soon as you finish reading this chapter. In order to get the most out of an attorney-client relationship, you must have read the recommended books and have a basic grasp of music business terminology. *But there will be times you need legal counsel.* Here is my own rule of thumb for deciding when:

> *Should you have an opportunity to place a song with an artist who has recognition beyond the local level, it is crucial that you seek competent legal counsel from an attorney who specializes in music and entertainment matters.*

> *Please don't consult your local personal injury or divorce attorney! They probably will not understand the intricacies of the music business or be competent to advise you in matters affecting the use and licensing of songs.*

Can't I Just Find Someone To Do All This Business Stuff For Me?

The entire premise of this book is that it is possible to succeed in the music business and to make money as a songwriter with or without the aid of a professional music publisher. You—the songwriter and owner of the song or copyright—are the publisher for the songs you write *unless* or *until* you sign a contract with another publisher.

Many right-brained creative types wish it were possible to sign a lifetime contract with an honest, loyal, zealous and hugely successful publisher whose sole desire is to see them succeed. The publisher might take care of all the business matters and let the writer concentrate on creating hits. Sometimes that happens. (Sometimes people win the lottery too.) But as I said at the very beginning of this book, your success will depend on how willing you are to accept responsibility for your own songs and your own musical destiny.

> *Songwriter ignorance in the area of music pub-*
> *lishing causes professional and financial train*
> *wrecks resulting in lost careers and lost fortunes.*

If you must act as your own publisher because you have no other options, that's not such a bad thing. You will be forced to learn the ropes for yourself and this may prove a great advantage in the end. Heck, if you've read this far, you already know a lot more than many successful music publishers did when they got started. So let's press on!

All Right...All Right...What's Next?

As you will recall from our discussion in chapter two, when the last note and word of a song have been fixed on paper or in a recording of any kind, you as the writer(s) own the whole song. If there is more than one writer involved, the percentages of ownership should be decided at the time of writing. (We will have more to say about co-writing in chapter six).

Many metaphors have been used to explain the concept of song ownership, some more helpful than others. One common analogy is that of the song as a pie. The trouble with this one is that it means different things to different people, some of whom know a good deal more about music—and about baking pies—than others. I may not be the world's greatest authority on music publishing but—fortunately for you—I can make a hell of a pie! So here is my pie maker's attempt at an explanation.

Of Pies and Publishing

If you and a friend or friends decide to bake a pie together, you first get out a big bowl and start dumping in the ingredients. One person measures and pours in the flour…another the salt…another the shortening etc. Then you have to stir all the ingredients together into a big lump. From this point on, none of the ingredients can be separated out. It is now a piecrust…or if you're still with me, it is now a song that has been fixed on paper or in audio form and is protected by copyright law. (If you're not still with me, go back and reread the above paragraph until you get the hang of it—or go watch an episode of Martha Stewart!)

You and your friends co-own that lump of dough since you each contributed ingredients that were used to form the whole. But now, let's suppose we want to make that one lump of dough into two pies. We separate it accordingly into two balls and roll them each flat. We will call one of them the *Writer's Pie* and the other the *Publisher's Pie*, but we bear in mind they are both parts of the original lump.

Each circle of pie dough is now considered 100 percent. You and your friend(s) will own the agreed-upon percentages for each pie because at this point, you are both the writers and the publishers. In essence you own 200 percent because you own both pies. Of course that 200 percent is really only 100 percent of the original lump of dough.

OK…I know you're lost, but just go back and read it again. Or, if necessary, bake a pie and study it that way. Once you get it, it ain't all that hard to keep it straight.

What is a Songwriter's Agreement ... And How Does It Affect The Pie?

Suppose that you make contact with a publisher who wants to sign a single song songwriter's agreement with you and your co-writers. When you sign the contract, you transfer ownership of the entire lump of dough to the publisher with the understanding that you will receive the *Writer's Pie* of any future profits. The publisher now owns the copyright and receives the *Publisher's Pie* in profits.

If you are the only writer, you will receive 100 percent of the *Writer's Pie*. If other writers are involved, you will share the writers' income based on percentages agreed upon previously. You and any other writers will not, however, own the song (the copyright) until the term of the agreement with your publisher has expired—which, unless otherwise stipulated—is seventy years after the death of the last surviving writer. In other words, you no longer own the lump of pie dough, but you can still eat the *Writer's Pie*. The agreement is binding—until seventy years after you have gone on to Songwriters' Heaven (a whole new meaning for the phrase "pie in the sky").

Incidentally, the "unless otherwise stipulated" phrase above refers to something called a *reversion clause* which, if included in the agreement, allows for the ownership of the copyright to revert to the writer(s) under certain conditions. We'll have more to say about this later.

The moral of the story is this:

> *Be careful with whom you bake because you'll
> be sharing your pie with them for a long time.*

Can You Give Me An Example?

Because these music biz basics are not well understood by most songwriters, mega-confusion results in the excitement of receiving that long-awaited songwriting contract. To illustrate, let's construct a scenario:

By now, you may already be the best-known songwriter in Boondocks. (After all, you have been reading and applying everything in this book, right?) You're itching to get your songs out there where they can become the blockbuster hits you know they are destined to be.

At your family reunion, you discover to your delight that your cousin, Frank, has a brother-in-law who once had a neighbor (now deceased) whose nephew drove a bus for Reba McIntyre back in the 80s. Cousin Frank is able to pull some strings and get you the address of a music publisher in Nashville who is accepting unsolicited material. You send in your carefully written, professionally demoed and beautifully packaged song. Much to your delight, John Q. Mogul, a representative of Showbiz Music Publishing—likes your song and sends you a single song songwriter agreement.

Without really understanding what you're signing, you believe that now, at last, you have become a published songwriter. You sit back in your recliner waiting for the checks to roll in. What you failed to realize is that the songwriting agreement you signed did not mean your song was published. It simply gave Showbiz Music ownership of your song and the right to try to get it published.

According to the Copyright Act, a song is not published until there has been:

♫   *distribution of copies or phono records of a work to the public by sale...*

OR

♫   *an offering to distribute copies or phonorecords to a group of persons for purposes of further distribution, public performance or public display.*

Hopefully, John Q. Mogul uses all his contacts in the business to promote and publish your song, but until the song is recorded and distributed for sale—or until there has been an offering to distribute it, the song remains unpublished and makes neither you nor Showbiz Music any money at all.

It is at this point that the importance of the reversion clause comes into play. You would hope the publisher would do everything in its power to promote the songs in its catalog. But sometimes, things don't quite work out that way.

Back to you in Boondocks...Mr. Mogul sincerely likes your song and believes he can get it cut. He's excited about the song's possibilities and is committed to its success. But several months after the contract is signed, Mr. Mogul leaves his position to go to work for another publishing company. Your song remains the property of Showbiz Music. (That's another thing about the music industry—the turnover in personnel at the various companies tends to run high.)

When a new employee arrives at Showbiz Music to take John Q's place, she knows nothing about you—or your song—and has no personal commitment to either. Months and years go by and you see no activity on your song. Without a reversion clause in your contract stipulating that you regain ownership of your song within a reasonable time, it may lie on the bottom of a file drawer at Showbiz and stagnate until seventy years after you have gone on to your reward. That's a long time!

Of course, you can continue to use whatever personal contacts and resources you have to pitch your song to artists and record labels. If and when you get a cut, Showbiz Music (the company that did nothing to promote your song) still owns the copyright and receives 100 percent of the publisher's share of income according to the songwriting agreement.

Are you beginning to see why a basic understanding of the music business is so critical? The old adage—*All that glitters is not gold*—has never been truer than it is in the world of entertainment. Let me say it once more:

> *Ultimately, the responsibility of getting your song to the world belongs to you!*

If you choose to enter into an agreement with a publisher, *be sure* you understand both the advantages and the pitfalls that may lie ahead. There are many kinds of publishers. Independent publishing companies run the gamut from very small to very large. Some publishing companies are owned by record labels. You do have choices. Make them wisely!

Get competent legal counsel to review any agreement you are offered before you sign anything.

If I Do Sign An Agreement With A Publisher What May I Realistically Expect?

You should not expect the publisher to be your business partner.

Many songwriters mistakenly think that the songwriter's agreement makes them a partner with the publisher in the ownership of a song, but this is not the case. As stated above, the publisher now owns the entire song. You stand to benefit from the publisher's expertise and contacts. Ideally your publisher finds ways for your song to earn money. If your publisher succeeds, you will receive the writer's share of any profits generated. It may help to think of the publisher as a *trustee* and yourself as a *beneficiary.*

You should expect your publisher to try hard to promote your song

It's the publisher's job to protect the copyright and exploit every opportunity for the song to earn income (it is in everyone's best interest for your song to become a hit). But the songwriting agreement is really a speculative collaboration. There is no guarantee that the publisher will be able to earn the first cent of income on your song. If the publisher is not able to make your song turn a profit, she has no obligation to pay you anything at all.

You should expect easy access to your publisher

It is important that you have a good, professional relationship with your publishing company and are able to contact them regularly to discuss your song(s) and what is being done to exploit the copyright(s) and generate income. The company may assign a certain key person to you—someone who is familiar with you as a writer and with your songs. Do your part to establish a friendly working relationship with that person so that you are kept abreast of any activity on your song(s) and so that the publisher does not forget you exist.

You should expect the publisher to obtain co-writing opportunities for you

Remember that a good publisher is also a mentor who helps you cultivate and hone your skills as a writer. One of the best ways for you to develop your skills is by co-writing with other (hopefully, more established) writers from whom you may learn the fine points of the craft and gain recognition as a professional. And co-writes may help to maximize the earning potential of a song...more about this in chapter 6.

You should not expect—but you should lobby hard for— a reversion clause in your contract

The songwriter's agreement may or may not contain a reversion clause. We touched on this important matter earlier. A reversion clause stipulates that if, after a certain period of time (the length of which is totally negotiable), the publishing company has been unsuccessful in its attempts to get the song published or recorded, the copyright reverts to the writer. In years past most songwriting contracts contained a reversion clause as a standard part of the agreement, but you should not expect one to be automatically included today!

Publishers, of course, would rather not have such a clause in the agreement because it usually takes considerable time and effort to get a song cut. It often requires as many as 100 pitches to place just one song on a record. They prefer not to have the pressure of an approaching reversion as they research opportunities and conduct promotions to get the song published.

On the other hand, it is usually in the songwriter's best interest to request a reversion clause even when you trust your publisher implicitly—to protect against unforeseen eventualities that are out of everyone's control. For example, your small publisher may become ill or retire and sell her entire catalog to a third party who may not believe in your song. Or, as we noted earlier, there may be personnel changes in the publishing company that mean your song is overlooked or forgotten. Remember that you will not get the copyright back in your lifetime unless there is some kind of reversion clause.

As you discuss this matter with your publisher, be reasonable and rational. Try to negotiate a reversion *term* that will work for both of you. A reversion clause may allow your publisher as few as two years or as many as ten (or more) to get the song published. The reversion clause is a safety net that protects you, the songwriter, against the possibility of a stalemate situation.

You are a professional. Act professionally. Don't assume that your prospective publisher is a shark just because there is no reversion clause in the contract. But stand up for your song and your own best interests. Remember that the reversion clause only applies if the publisher fails to get your song published or recorded within a specific time frame. If the publisher is successful and the song is published, the reversion clause is moot and the song belongs to the publisher for the life of the copyright.

You should not expect any money to change hands at the signing of a single song agreement

As stated earlier, the single song agreement is based on a belief in the song's future revenues. There is usually no money exchanged in the signing of this agreement. If the song requires a professional demo, the publisher will usually absorb that expense. As a new writer, you should not be expected to pay any upfront costs yourself, nor should you expect to receive any royalties—until the publisher is successful in generating income with your song from recordings, print publications, performances etc.

You can expect to reimburse the publisher for certain costs

Although your publisher will usually pay for any costs required to demo your song, you may be required to reimburse the publisher for those expenses somewhere along the line. If, for instance, your songwriter's agreement contains a reversion clause and you choose to exercise your option to reclaim the copyright, you will probably be expected to reimburse the publisher for any demo expenses incurred on your song during the term of the contract. Even if you stay with the publisher and your song begins to earn money, you may still be required to repay demo expenses from your earnings.

You should not expect a salary

With established and proven writers or with staff songwriters who are under contract to write exclusively for music companies, publishers may agree to pay an advance. But this is not to be confused with a salary. An advance is simply a loan against your future royalties that will be recouped from your song's income later on.

Does Size Really Matter?
Or...What Are The Pros And Cons Of Smaller Publishers?

There are many well-respected, small boutique publishing houses with influential industry contacts and lots of credibility. Some small publishers, however, may have fewer contacts and fewer employees. This can mean fewer opportunities to pitch your songs to major artists. As you have been learning, the responsibility for researching your options belongs to you.

Smaller independent publishers can frequently offer aspiring songwriters more individual time and attention. A good publisher (who may be a songwriter herself) can be an invaluable asset to a new diamond-in-the-rough songwriter who may be very gifted but still requires polishing on the fine points of the craft.

If you are approached by a small publisher who is interested in your song(s), think carefully about your career. What is the next right thing for you?

If you are already an accomplished songwriter and are confident that your songs are bulletproof hits, you may want to shoot for a larger publisher. If, however, you are a novice songwriter, you may be very wise to accept a contract from a smaller, more approachable publisher who really believes in you and your music and is prepared to help coach you to greatness. And remember, even if both you and your publisher are relatively unknown, it only takes one big hit to make both of you into stars.

What About Large Publishers?

Large publishers, of course, have high prestige and many contacts.

Back in the early 1960s a songwriter named Roger Miller wrote his really big hit—a song called "King of the Road". The song was signed to Sony Music Publishing, one of the largest publishing houses in the country. Today, decades after it was written, "King of the Road" is still making money for Sony and for Roger Miller's heirs—all because of the aggressive activity of Sony Publishing on behalf of the song. Through Sony's contacts with major corporations and artists, "King of the Road" has been used in commercials for a variety of products—from hamburgers to trucks. It has been recorded or covered by countless artists besides Roger Miller—including Randy Travis, Boxcar Willie, Ray Coniff, REM and even the Chipmunks! And every time you hear it…kaching!

After hearing a success story like Roger Miller's, it is extremely tempting to hold out for a publishing deal from a mega corporation. But there are, of course, disadvantages to signing with major companies. If you are a new and relatively unproven songwriter who has just signed a song with a large company, you and your song may be buried in their huge catalog.

A big publishing company has many contacts and lots of clout that might theoretically be exploited to promote your song, but it may give your song little or no priority because it is busy with more established writers. Even with a contract from a major company, your song may never see the light of day.

What If I Just Keep Acting As My Own Publisher?

Having weighed both the above options, you may decide to continue to do-it-yourself and act as your own music publisher rather than to forfeit any of your song's earnings. It is not difficult to establish your own music publishing company.

> *All that is required to create your own company is that you register with the same performing rights organization that you joined as a writer—but this time, you will register as a publisher. You will be asked to name your company (actually this is the hardest part of the process because so many good names have already been taken). You may also be required to register your business with your local government as a DBA (Doing Business As). And that's really all there is to becoming a full-blown publisher.*

Once you have a publishing company of your own, you can identify all your songs (lyric sheets, lead sheets, and demo CDs) with your name, the name of your publishing company and the year the song was written. Your copyright symbol should be presented like this:

Words and Music by Joe Smith
©2007 JoeSmithMusic

You will inevitably run into the same challenges every small, independent publisher faces (see above). But you'll learn a lot about the industry and as your own publisher, you'll have a *personal* stake in your catalog. You'll be sure to give your songs the time and energy required to succeed.

What Is Co-Publishing And How Does It Work?

Having your own publishing company will allow you more creative and promotional control over your songs, and you can still enter into agreements with larger publishers as a co-publisher. Co-publishing means that you and the other publisher will divide the *Publisher's Pie* according to agreed-upon percentages in your co-publishing contract and will co-own the copyright. Co-publishers share the expense and the workload—and any profits realized—for pitching the song to artists. As co-publisher, you have the advantage of access to the larger publisher's contacts while retaining a percentage of the ownership of your song.

Recall that you can only join one of the performing rights organizations as a writer. As a publisher, however, you may decide to represent songs by other writers who belong to other PROs. Since songwriters must sign agreements with publishers that belong to the same PRO they do, you as a publisher may decide to establish separate publishing companies in all three PROs so that you can sign songs by any writer you wish. This allows you to add to your catalog of songs and increases the likelihood of your having the right song for that superstar artist that needs a blockbuster single.

That's the way this thing works. It is, incidentally, the way small music companies become monster conglomerates.

As You Decide...

Whichever option you choose—small, large or self-publishing—remember that you as the songwriter must continue to accept responsibility for your song(s). If you have signed a songwriter's agreement with a publisher and you haven't heard from them in a month, call or write to find out where the publisher has pitched your song and what response it has had. Make sure your publisher knows you exist by staying in touch and being persistent. Position yourself just a few degrees shy of obnoxious in your follow-up. As they say, it's the squeaky wheel that gets the grease!

If you decide to start your own publishing company and take the DIY approach, decide now that you will be the kind of publisher your great songs deserve. This will mean that you master the business of music as well as the art of networking so that you, as a publisher, will have the contact base necessary to maximize the profitability and impact of your copyrights. There is no shortcut here, but you will meet the most interesting people in the world and receive an education in life as well as in business.

Hey Wait A Minute...You Promised To Explain What It Means To Sell A Song And What A Work-for-Hire Is!

You're right. I promised, so here's the skinny…

You may choose to sell a song outright under a work-for-hire agreement, but please realize that this is a high voltage area. Beware of loose wires. In a work-for-hire you, the writer, are typically compensated for the song or composition with a one-time payment. You then sacrifice all future income and recognition the song may generate. In fact, the person or company who bought your song may now claim authorship. You have just "sold your child."

The two most common scenarios for a work-for-hire are:

Works Prepared by Employees

When a songwriter signs an exclusive agreement to become a staff song-writer for a publisher, the agreement may contain wording to the effect that all songs written by the songwriter are works-for-hire. In other words, the publisher is now the sole owner of all songs (copyrights) created by the writer during the term of the agreement. This is completely legal according to the 1976 Copyright Law and means that the publisher can claim authorship of the song without any credit being given the actual songwriter.

Incidentally, the term of a work-for-hire agreement is not seventy years after the death of the last surviving songwriter as it is in a songwriter's agreement, but 95 years from the date of publication or 120 years from the date of creation—whichever expires first.

To be fair we note that most publishers who include a work-for-hire clause in a staff songwriting contract will agree to credit the writer and pay the usual writer's royalties. But your stake now depends upon your publisher's good will (or lack thereof). If the publisher decides to claim complete authorship, this is entirely within the law. It is often prudent to avoid any kind of work-for-hire language in a staff songwriter agreement. This is where you really need a competent lawyer to watch your back.

Commissioned Works

Sometimes a company or an individual commissions a songwriter to create a song for a specific use—usually for an event of some kind such as a charity drive or special banquet—and offers to buy the composition outright. You may have the chance to place your song in an independent film or write a jingle for a one-time payment—waiving future royalties.

Occasionally, the payment is large enough and the future of the song is limited enough to warrant a one-time payment. Once again I caution you to be sure you understand the many facets of such an agreement and obtain expert legal advice before you enter into it.

Under the work-for-hire, you have sold your intellectual property for cash. You will have no further claim to it.

CONCLUSION

There sure is a lot to learn about the business of music.

The information we have covered here is extremely basic and should not be substituted for in-depth reading on the subject or professional legal counsel. A good entertainment attorney is invaluable for protecting your intellectual property and helping you to gain contacts in the industry.

I do hope this chapter has helped familiarize you with some of the concepts and terms used in the business of music. I hope too that you have begun to see the importance of music publishing and the myriad opportunities and pitfalls it opens on the road to success. Determine to keep educating yourself by reading and studying a little at a time.

In the last analysis, you as the writer of the song and the song's original publisher must take responsibility for every opportunity that comes your way. You'll sometimes be required to walk a very narrow precipice between two equally dangerous dropoffs—avarice and paranoia on the one side, naiveté and gullibility on the other.

Only you can answer the question: Deal…or no deal?

REWIND...

~ Besides acting as mentor/coach for the songwriter, a music publisher must also be a promoter of the songs in her catalog.

~ To adequately promote a song, one must understand how songs make money and the importance of copyright ownership.

~ Learn the basics of the music business by reading good books on the subject, but don't neglect to obtain specialized legal counsel when necessary.

~ Understand what you are signing before you sign.

6

Co-Writing and Common Sense

Co-Writing, a Personal Reflection

I began my songwriting career at age three or four writing songs with my dad at the piano. He was not a trained musician, but he had a wonderful ear. He would plop me down at the treble end of the piano and I would pick out melodies while he pounded out chords on the bass end. I don't remember any of the songs we wrote, but I sure remember how much fun we had! That was my introduction to co-writing.

When I was older I continued to write songs but without a collaborator. Sitting at the piano, I would start with a chord progression or melody and then find words to go with the music. I wrote some pretty good songs that way, but I always felt a bit limited because I was better at lyrics than music.

When I attended my first songwriting conference I heard a great deal about co-writing and decided to give it a try. After a couple of not-so-positive attempts to write songs with other writers, I met a brilliant musician who believed me to be an accomplished lyricist. We clicked. The result was amazing for both of us. Each of us had creative talents, but together they were multiplied a thousand fold. Over the next five years we wrote more than 200 songs together. I have been co-writing ever since.

Today, I have the privilege of writing with gifted composers from all parts of the country and in all genres of music. Most of my writing partners have become close friends, but I sometimes write on assignment with composers I don't even know. I still write my own songs at the piano as I always have, but I have come to realize that my strong suit is crafting lyrics, so in most co-writing arrangements I write the words.

Co-writing songs has been a wonderful experience for me and has taught me as much about the music business as it has about relationships in general. I've learned that there is lot more to co-writing than writing a song.

What Are Some Of The Perks Of Co-Writing?

There are many wonderful facets of co-writing. I'll list just a few:

Co-Writing is Just Plain Fun

There's something magical about getting together with someone else as flaky as you are and creating a wonderful song together.

Sometimes it happens spontaneously—two writers sitting down together in a room over a cup of coffee. One writer may come up with an idea. The other offers a great hook/title to hang the idea on and then things just start to happen. Bands practicing together often stumble upon a chord progression or riff that evolves into a melody and lyrics—and *voila!* A hit song is born.

Sometimes songwriting appointments are planned. An artist may be looking for a particular style of song with a certain message. You and your co-writer(s) may meet with the expressed purpose of writing that song. However it happens, when you walk away a few hours (or days or weeks) later with something terrific that you have helped to create, there is a high only a song-writer knows.

Co-Writing Provides Immediate Feedback

Co-writers who are able to overcome the initial awkwardness of their relationship learn to interact with each other honestly. You have an idea you think is absolutely stupid, but when you take the plunge and share it, you find that your co-writer considers it genius. (Or not!)

With a little thick skin and a good sense of humor, you and your writing partner will learn to exchange ideas transparently, quickly selecting the best and discarding the rest. This creative interchange proves the old adage that "two heads are better than one."

Co-Writers Share Responsibility for Promoting the Song

The songs we co-write are like our kids. Parental duties don't end when the song (or kid) is birthed. That's only the beginning. If you and your writing partner co-own both the writer's and publisher's shares of the song, you will also share the work and expense of giving that kid (or song) the best opportunity to succeed.

What exactly does this entail? You already know most of it. You will need to create a professional demo and presentation package as described in chapters three and four—only this time you will have a partner to help you. As co-writers, and acting as your own publishers, you will share the expense of creating the demo. You will also divide the effort required to promote the song.

Divisions of the workload sometimes happen naturally. For example, I co-write with many wonderful musicians who are also accomplished producers and have great voices. My co-writer may agree to produce and record the demo for our song, while I (the more technologically challenged member of the team) create the presentation package and register the copyright. Each of us combs our own database of contacts for pitch opportunities. The inspiration required to get the song out there where it has a chance of being heard and recorded is multiplied, just as the creativity was when the song was being written.

As "parents" we want to do whatever it takes to ensure the "kids" have the best shot at achieving their full potential. We watch as these wonderful creations of ours take on lives of their own and end up in places we never would have dreamed. Some kids leave home never to be heard from again. Others, you hope no one ever knows are yours. And then some kids make you proud.

Co-Writing Offers Each Writer a Chance to Expand Her Knowledge of the Craft

In chapter one we discussed the importance of finding collaborators—especially if you write just music or only lyrics. If you, as a skilled lyricist, team up with a wonderful composer/musician, I promise that you'll learn something about music in the process and that your partner will learn something about lyrics.

As you branch out, networking within your Boondocks Music Community, you'll meet skilled writers of Country, Pop, Blues—or even Musical Theater. Offer to collaborate with these writers, even if their genre is something you have never tried. You're already learning volumes about the craft of songwriting by having every button on your car radio tuned to a different style of music. You will also gain invaluable experience every time you try your hand at songwriting in a new genre. With each co-write, you become a more skilled and multi-faceted professional. All the while you will be building a large and varied catalog of songs that draws artists looking for original material.

Co-Writing "Up" Can Advance Your Career

If you continue to improve and excel as a songwriter, you may one day find yourself collaborating with a nationally recognized songwriter or artist. Don't think it can't happen from Boondocks! I am living proof it can.

In order to capitalize on such opportunities you must learn to evaluate your work objectively. It is not uncommon for a beginning writer—caught up in the rush of creating her first songs—to believe each new song she writes is her best ever. With time and experience, she learns to detach from her work enough to critique her own songs. She uses the solid grasp of songwriting craftsmanship she has earned to evaluate her work. She knows she is turning out lots of good songs on a regular basis. But...every once in a while she comes up with a melody or a lyric fragment—or she has an idea— she knows (and not just hopes) is a hit in the making.

If this has happened to you, you know how tempting it can be to call on one of your regular co-writers to help you complete the song. Be sure to think strategically before you do. Even if your co-writer is a master at the craft and the song turns out exceptionally well, you need to ask yourself: do you (as the parents of this new kid) have the contacts and resources to make it into the worldwide hit it has the potential to become? Or is it destined to be yet another great song no one ever hears because neither you nor your co-writer have the marketing or promotional connections required for success?

> *You may be wise to keep some song nuggets tucked away in a safe place. When the chance comes to pitch a song idea to a major writer, you'll have some little treasures on hand.*

Should you have an opportunity to write with someone from the major leagues, be sure you have some of your best work to present.

OK...What Are The Pitfalls In Co-Writing?

As in any exciting relationship, there are downs as well as ups. Because co-writing can be so exhilarating, many songwriters lose their footing in the emotional high of the process and neglect the business implications of song ownership (the parental duties that follow). When these issues are not addressed before the fact, arguments and squabbles later erupt that can result in the breakup of bands or the ruin of otherwise magical collaborations.

Here are just a few potential difficulties:

Money

In my opinion, the greatest hazard to co-writing relationships is money. (The irony is that money incentivizes co-writing in the first place.) When cash appears, the writers involved in the creation of a song—as well as a few that weren't even there—can sometimes begin to think they did more than they really did and deserve more than they really do. I'm sure there is a scientific law that states:

As any song begins to generate income, the memories of the writers fuzz out exponentially.

Misunderstandings

Co-writing catastrophes often develop from faulty assumptions about the percentages of ownership and the plan to promote the song. Here are some possible scenarios:

♪ **You Assume that You are the Only Other Writer**
A friend may invite you to write a song with her. You mistakenly assume that you are the only other writer when, in fact, she has already begun to write the song with someone else. They have gotten a bit stuck in the writing process, so you have been invited to join them. Instead of a 50/50 split in the ownership of the copyright, this may mean that you are only going to receive 33 percent.

♪ **Another Writer is Invited into the Mix by Your Co-Writer**
In a variation of the scenario above, you are one of two original writers—then your co-writer invites in a third party to collaborate without asking you first.

♪ **You and Your Co-Writer Have Different Agendas for the Song**
Suppose you and a co-writer create a song together. You each own 50 percent of both the *Writer's* and *Publisher's Pies*. Now a major publisher with lots of clout appears who has an inside connection with a nationally recognized artist looking for a song like yours. The publisher is sure he can place it with the artist, but he insists on owning all of the publishing if he secures the cut. In other words, he wants to own the copyright—the entire publisher's share.

You are amenable to this offer because of the amazing credibility a major label cut would provide both you and your co-writer. You are of a mind that it is far better to have a small share of something big than a big one of little or nothing. But your writing partner will have none of this. She insists on keeping her 50 percent of the *Publisher's* and *Writer's Pies*. If she is unwilling to sign over her portion of the publishing to the major publisher, the opportunity will be lost.

♪ You Are Writing All the Songs for Your Band, but the Band Members Want to Be Included in the Song Ownership

I find emails describing one version or another of this scenario in my inbox nearly every day. One or two members of a band find they are writing all the band's original songs. The other members think they should be included as writers just because they are in the band.

♪ You Pay a Producer to Arrange and Sequence a Demo, Then the Producer wants to be Included as a Co-Writer

This is another very common dilemma. If you have written lyrics and a melody, you have created a song that is automatically protected by copyright law. You will recall that there is a small but very important word required for the protections stipulated under that law to kick in. The word is *fixed*. Your song needs to be expressed on music paper with lyrics, or in a simple audio recording, no matter how rough (even if you're just squawking into a box recorder a cappella) and marked with the copyright symbol, your name and date of composition.

If you fail to fix your original words and melody on paper or record them prior to hiring a producer to create an arrangement for your melody, you will have no real proof that the producer did not help you write your song. Later, the producer may claim to have co-written the song with you and demand a percentage of ownership.

These are just a few of the many conflicts that cause the breakup of talented co-writing partnerships before they achieve success. They can be avoided easily by asking questions and resolving disagreements *before* writing begins.

OK, So How Do I Avoid These Co-Writing Catastrophes?

This is where a little common sense, some honest communication and a sincere effort to apply the Golden Rule can help you navigate around co-writing landmines.

Clarify the Co-Writing Arrangement Upfront

If you are invited to co-write, don't be afraid to ask questions that define the arrangement with the other writers before the fact. Questions like:

♪ *Who is involved in this co-write? Just you and I—or are there others?*

♪ *How will the percentages of ownership be divided among the writers?*

♪ *What is our plan for this song once it is written?*

♪ *Are we all willing to sacrifice equal parts of our publisher's share to a larger publishing or record company in order to secure a major cut?*

Have an Open Conversation with the Co-Writer(s) at the Time of Writing

This is extremely important—especially if you are in a new co-writing relationship or in a band that writes original music.

As mentioned earlier, collaboration often occurs spontaneously between friends, or among band mates at a rehearsal. The excitement of creating a new song frequently eclipses the question of song ownership. Nobody is even thinking about songwriting splits in the high of the moment. Sometimes those splits can't realistically be determined until the song is finished. The fact remains that an honest discussion among the principals about the ownership of their song is a must—and the sooner the better.

Remember: A song is considered copyrighted at the moment the last note and word are fixed. For it to be considered fixed it must either be recorded using audio equipment or written down on paper. It is then protected whether the song is registered immediately with the US Copyright Office or not. Unless there are publishers involved, the songwriters own the entire pie—the publisher's share AND the writers' share.

The pies can be sliced as thinly or thickly as desired. The important thing is that all the writers are satisfied with their slices.

One writer may contribute an idea and hook/title for a song, while two other writers pen words and a melody. In this scenario, the three may agree that the contributor of the idea deserves 10-15 percent of the song and that the remaining percentage should be divided equally between the others. Since the two who wrote the words and melody did most of the work, they may well deserve the lion's share of the ownership. If, however, the idea/hook is a killer—a sure-fire, slam-dunk, original piece of genius—the writers may decide that its importance is worth an equal share and decide to divide the copyright in thirds.

When band members write together, one person may come up with a unique musical riff or guitar lick. That may be his only contribution. But if that two-bar piece of music becomes the musical signature for the song, its value may warrant a larger portion of ownership because it is integral to the song's total impact. (Consider the amazing bass riff in the famous song, *Message in a Bottle* by the Police. How much would you be willing to give up for that?)

Some band members show little interest in the writing of a song and contribute little to its creation. When the song is finished they may feel they deserve an equal share just for being members of the band. Perhaps they do—especially if you see a future for the band as a whole and want to keep everyone happy. Perhaps not! The writing members may decide that the others are riding the coattails of their hard work.

Again, these are decisions that only you (and your co-writers) can make. Don't sweep them under the "flying carpet" known as the songwriters' high. They won't go away if you ignore them. They will only erupt later with greater risk of loss.

Draw Up a Simple Co-Writers' Letter of Agreement

It is imperative—when the song is newly written and the songwriting specifics are fresh in each writer's mind—that all those involved have an honest and realistic conversation about the song's percentages. If it is a simple co-write with one writer composing the melody and the other writing the lyrics, the split is typically 50/50. If, however, there are more than two writers, the splits are entirely negotiable. There are no hard and fast rules for determining each writer's percentage of ownership, but it is essential that everyone involved reach a single agreement.

When possible base the percentages on the extent and importance of each writer's contribution.

Are you starting to see why it's so important to be frank, and in agreement about these things *before the fact?* Once the writers have agreed to the percentages and split the shares of the song, they can formalize their consent in a simple letter of agreement. This letter does not have to be a threatening twenty-page legal document. A clear statement containing the names of the writers, the date of composition, the percentage of ownership for each, and a statement of intent for the promotion of the song will suffice.

Copies of the letter should be made for each writer with all copies signed by all writers (no photocopies of signatures). Each participating writer should have a copy of the letter, signed by all, for her records. It is wise to have an extra copy in safekeeping with an attorney or trusted party as a safeguard.

For a sample Letter of Agreement between co-writers, see Appendix C.

Clarify and Document Agreements with Demo Producers

Whether you decide to use a demo producer in Boondocks, or one located in a far away music capital like Nashville, be sure that you understand and document the agreement between you and the producer before she begins creating your song demos. Most demo production services for beginning songwriters are done strictly on a work-for-hire basis. You will remember this term from chapter five when we discussed how it relates to copyright ownership. The rules are nearly the same when applied to demo production:

> *You, the songwriter(s), agree with the producer on a one-time fee to be paid for each song you wish her to arrange and produce. This will include the sequencing, arranging, studio and mixing time. There may be extra costs associated with hiring background singers or live musicians. When these fees are paid, the producer has no further claim to the demo or the song.*

Most demo producers who work with unknown and aspiring songwriters charge on a per song basis. This should be stated clearly in a letter of agreement signed by both the writer(s) and the producer prior to the first session. The cost for demo singers and live musicians provided by the producer may be included in the letter of agreement. Or you may need to create separate agreements for each singer and musician involved. Work out these details at the beginning. The harmonies and rhythms that the producer adds, are paid for in the production fee and do not give her a legal claim to ownership of any part of your song.

Nationally recognized producers may require percentage points of copyright ownership if a recording is to be sold or if it is to receive major airplay, but this does not usually apply to demo producers who are paid by aspiring songwriters to create demonstration recordings of their songs. The important thing here, as in all collaborations, is that everyone involved is on the same page to prevent misunderstanding after the demo is underway or finished.

I recently received an email from a writer who was producing her very first three demos. She had contracted with a producer to create the recordings at $500 per song. The producer added harmonies and rhythms and arranged the songs. The writer paid additional fees for the studio singers. After the demos were finished, the producer sent her a legal document insisting on 50 percent ownership and claiming to have co-written the songs.

This kind of fiasco can be easily avoided before the fact with a letter of agreement. Without a formal agreement you may well be headed for the School of Hard Knocks unless you can prove you wrote both words and melody prior to engaging the producer's services. To ensure legal protection, it is wise to register your songs with the US Copyright Office before any production work is undertaken—especially if you are engaging producers you haven't worked with in the past.

For a sample Letter of Agreement between songwriters and demo producers, refer to Appendix C.

Be Informed About Common Co-Writing Practices in Music Capitals

In strong music communities like Nashville where songwriting is an industry all its own, co-writes take place between staff writers from different publishing companies all the time. Because there are so many professional songwriters interacting every day to create intellectual property, Nashville has developed an equal share system where anyone who even happens to be in the room at the time of writing shares the writers' credits—no matter how marginal the contribution. (Urban legend has it that a few potted plants have received writer's percentages because they happened to be in the right place at the right time.)

If you have the good fortune to pursue collaboration in Nashville, you will be among some of the greatest songwriters in the world (most of whom are very nice people to boot). Just be aware of the equal share system and inquire about the method used to divide the credits and copyrights before your co-writing appointment. If you are aware and informed first, you are unlikely to be unpleasantly surprised later.

If you are an independent writer collaborating with a staff songwriter from a major publishing house, don't make the mistake of thinking that your portion of the *Publisher's Pie* now automatically belongs to your collaborator's publishing company—even if the publisher is a big and powerful one. As a staff songwriter, your co-writer will receive only a writer's share of the earnings because the publishing company will own her share of the copyright. You, as an independent, continue to act as your own publisher. Unless or until you sign an agreement to the contrary, you own your publisher's share of the copyright as well as your writer's share.

You may decide that it would be in your long-term advantage to surrender your share of the publishing to the larger company. Doing so may help you get your foot in the door and create the good will necessary for future opportunities. Just remember that you have a valuable asset in your percentage of the copyright. Negotiate it prudently.

Did You Mention Something Earlier About the Golden Rule?

Yes, I did, and it can make all the difference in the world.

The two most important components of a songwriter's reputation are *skill* and *integrity*.

Collaborators will be attracted to you by your skill as a songwriter, but they will continue with you because of your integrity. Settle for nothing less than excellence in your craft, and then make it your policy to treat each co-writer as you yourself would like to be treated. Let that policy guide your conduct during the writing of the song and the work required afterwards.

Maintain good communication with your co-writer(s) as you would with any good friend. If you are the more experienced writer, set the pace by being open and by encouraging your partner to share her ideas—no matter how zany. If you are the junior member of the team, be respectful and teachable, but step up to the plate and add your thoughts confidently. Remember that you are partners. Work together amicably. Don't take liberties with the song (changing it drastically, inviting someone else to collaborate etc.) without talking to your co-writer first.

What If I've Already Blown It In A Co-Writing Relationship?

You may have been the cause of a band breakup or the ruin of an otherwise wonderful co-writing relationship through your own naiveté and miscalculation. Perhaps you're the one who has been wounded or cheated by someone else's unethical behavior. Whatever the case, don't lose heart.

There is not a serious songwriter on the planet who couldn't fill your ear with stories of lost royalties, wasted effort, betrayals and monumental goof ups. Try not to get stuck in the quicksand of regret and don't get hung up over that song that didn't become the hit it should have been. Practice a little humility. Accept responsibility when you are in the wrong and apologize. Forgive easily. Move on!

If you are into songwriting for the long haul, you must learn to take a broad view of the landscape. Cultivate a little philosophical detachment. You have better songs in you than that one you lost. Don't get bitter—get better. Move on to the next challenge. The best is always yet to come!

CONCLUSION

Co-writing is one of the best parts of the songwriter's journey. Twenty-first century technology is opening new connections and allowing for the cross pollination of talent as never before. Don't be afraid to step out and attempt new co-writes. Stretch yourself. Grow.

Whatever you do, however, and with whomever you decide to collaborate, cover yourself with paper. Simply make it a practice to put in writing what you and any collaborator have verbally agreed to. Good housekeeping procedures don't threaten relationships—they clarify them. Robert Frost once wisely observed that:

Good fences make good neighbors[1]

Or as my old college English Lit professor used to say:
verbum sat sapienti
"A word to the wise is sufficient."

Rewind...

~ Co-writing is one of the great adventures in song-writing—filled with both perks and pitfalls.

~ Co-writing multiplies the fun of songwriting and divides the work.

~ Misunderstandings and mistaken assumptions can cause the collapse of otherwise brilliant collaborations.

~ Be sure that you and the other writer(s) are in agreement before the fact about the ownership of any songs you write and your vision for them.

~ Develop your reputation as a co-writer through skill and integrity.

[1] Frost, Robert; *Mending Wall*, 1914

NOTES

PART TWO

LIFTING THE
BARRIERS

CHAPTERS 7-12

7

The Times They Are A-Changin'

You now know just enough to be dangerous!

The first six chapters of this book might be assigned in a course called *Remedial Songwriting 101.* Think of them as the *CliffsNotes* to some lengthier books on the music business. I hope you are already voraciously devouring the wonderful writings of Donald Passman, Jason Blume and Randy Poe. I also hope that you have received enough inspiration to get you off the couch and doing something about the music that burns in your heart.

In the remaining chapters of this book we will explore many new and exciting ways for you to wear your promoter's hat as a DIY publisher. Only don't forget your mentor's hat and its responsibilities as you move forward.

Be conscientious about your disciplined reading program (chapter two). Digest the latest and most reputable books from knowledgeable professionals on the subject of songwriting. Attend songwriting seminars. Stay abreast of the latest trends in music by reading recognized periodicals. Most of all, keep writing songs—songs that get consistently better and better each time. Promote your music, and remember to keep pushing yourself. As your own mentor/publisher the responsibility of perfecting your craft is yours and yours alone.

Believe me, I know how hard it can be—especially when you are a one-man-band—doing everything from songwriting…to booking…to gigging…to shipping…to janitorial duties. But there is no room for apathy in this deal. If you really want to be considered a credible and intelligent professional, there are no shortcuts. Don't rely on the half-correct, uninvestigated information of hobbyists passing themselves off as pros. Assume the responsibility of wearing both the mentor's hat and the promoter's hat. Wear them with intelligence and integrity. *Your goal is to become a full-fledged expert in every sense of the word.*

As we proceed, we'll venture upon new and uncharted territory without neglecting to explore the tried-and-true methods of the past. Anything goes these days! Whatever works is OK—as long as it doesn't get you arrested. Incredible changes taking place in the music industry and technological advances inconceivable just a few short years ago are revolutionizing what it means to succeed in this business.

Bob Dylan, the reluctant prophet of a generation, was never more prescient than when he penned these lyrics decades ago:

> *Come writers and critics*
> *Who prophesy with your pen*
> *And keep your eyes wide*
> *The chance won't come again*
> *And don't speak too soon*
> *For the wheel's still in spin*
> *And there's no tellin' who*
> *That it's namin'*
> *For the loser now*
> *Will be later to win*
> *For the times they are a changin'* [1]

I have been involved in many phases of the music industry for over twenty years. The first fifteen were spent learning how things are done in this business. The last several years have been spent un-learning them!

What Exactly Is Changing In The Music Business?

Toto, We're Not in Nashville Anymore

You remember the story. A tornado touches down in the middle of Kansas, and suddenly a young girl named Dorothy and her dog, Toto, are transported from a familiar Kansas landscape to the mysterious Land of Oz. Dorothy takes in her new surroundings with wonder. Although she isn't quite sure where she has ended up, she's dead sure she's no longer in Kansas!

Artists and songwriters who have been at this awhile can relate. Cherished theories and long-held beliefs about how one succeeds in music are being altered or made obsolete, almost on a daily basis. The landscape has definitely changed. Like Dorothy, many of us are asking, "Where the heck are we?"

The Way We Were

For most of the twentieth century it was believed real success meant signing a recording or publishing contract with a major music company. To have a decent shot, aspiring artists were encouraged to move to one of the three main music cities—LA, New York or Nashville—where (theoretically) it would be possible to develop relationships with music industry insiders who could "get you a deal" (meaning a record contract for artists or a staff writer position with a major music publisher for songwriters).

From the days of Tin Pan Alley through the early eighties this was more or less the way things were done. At first, it worked pretty well. Innovators were on the lookout for talented writers and musicians. It was not unusual for ambitious young songwriters to walk in off the street, play some songs for a publisher and walk out with a deal the same day. Competition between companies was healthy. The industry was young and hungry and opportunities were plentiful. When a promising new talent was found, publishers and producers invested time, effort and money to maximize her creative potential.

Although this mentor/mentee model for the relationship between music companies and their artists created some control and dependency issues, it worked pretty well for both sides. The music company would provide access to great studios with expensive high-tech recording equipment, skilled producers, and engineers. When the recording was finished, the company arranged for national distribution to all major retail outlets. All the writer or artist had to do was keep cranking out hits.

As the twentieth century drew to a close, music company mergers formed larger and larger corporations. The need to succeed financially became paramount. Pressure at the bottom line caused companies to focus their time and attention on proven artists who could ensure a profit at the cash register. Less and less time was spent searching out and mentoring new talent. Careers lived and died on the fickle whims of powerful music companies who cared less about talent and art than cold, hard returns. Aspiring artists continued to look to these corporations for the product distribution, studio facilities and tour support required for national success but many began to suspect they'd have better luck playing the lottery! Even songwriters and artists who followed the conventional wisdom, relocating to one of the music capitals with stars in their eyes, often returned home heartbroken.

How did lyricist Hal David put it?

> *L. A. is a great big freeway*
> *Put a hundred down and buy a car*
> *In a week - maybe two - they'll make you a star*
> *Weeks turn into years and quickly pass*
> *And all the stars that never were*
> *Are parkin' cars and pumpin' gas* [2]

What Happened Then?

The Mouse That Roared

It all began very quietly. As quiet as a mouse…only this mouse was attached to a computer!

I remember going to a music conference in 1990 where I attended a demonstration of a music notation software package called *Finale*. It was all very interesting, but it looked really hard—way over my head. I had recently purchased my first computer and had just learned how to turn it on. A gentleman sitting next to me must have noticed my bewildered expression. He nudged me and said, "Don't get one of these *Finale* gadgets now. Just wait a few years. They'll make it so simple even we can do it."

That man was right! Advances in technology have changed everything! Home computers are so affordable today that almost everyone has one or has access to one. Serious alternatives to the expensive digital recording equipment used in state-of-the-art studios now cram the shelves of your local computer retailer. Consumer-friendly software packages offer a world of instrumental sounds and sophisticated recording options with the convenience of a mouse click. With a little talent, some time in the learning curve and a bit of sweat equity novices can learn to produce recordings that compete with those of major music companies—and they can do it at a fraction of the cost.

The more artists and writers learn about creating and manufacturing their own CDs the less they depend on far away publishers. The traditional mentor/publisher figure of the past is being supplanted as songwriters all over the country begin to mentor each other through local songwriters' organizations. Members share their songwriting skills and their recording and computer knowledge the same way old-time music publishers once shared their expertise with staff songwriters. Computer technology is allowing writers and artists to compete in a way unheard of in times past. The playing field is being leveled.

Enter the Internet

Wow! If you thought things were changing fast before…you ain't seen nothin' yet!

Nothing in the history of the world has opened the floodgates quite like the Internet. Information is being disseminated at an unprecedented rate and to an extent that is scarcely conceivable. With the open transmission of data have come new channels for the distribution of products. Anybody anywhere can set up a cyber storefront and sell whatever they have to sell—to whomever may be looking. The success of Ebay has proven that somebody somewhere is looking for what somebody else is selling, no matter how strange or improbable the product.

Of course, as with any technology, you take the bad with the good. At first it was believed the World Wide Web would usher in a democratic revolution. Real power would be placed into the hands of the average person. Nobody anticipated annoyances like pop-up advertising and mountains of spam. Genuine perils such as privacy invasion, identity theft, and child endangerment were as yet unglimpsed. So, I am certainly not uncritically singing the praises of the Internet.

I am saying that for independent artists and writers, the Web has been a nearly unqualified boon. It has made possible instant worldwide distribution of product and has created entrepreneurial opportunities never before imagined. More amazing than anything else, the Internet is allowing people to collaborate with each other from opposite ends of the country and sometimes from opposite ends of the planet. Huge Internet songwriting communities enable writers to share information about the writing and promotion of songs. You can even enroll in songwriting courses with some of the best teachers in the world—all through the Internet.

Opening the Barn Door

The music industry began to feel the first tremors of the Internet tsunami as the twentieth century drew to a close. The old paradigm—a few mega-companies monopolizing the music market—began to quiver. Artists and writers who had given up hope of national exposure and distribution saw an opportunity to take responsibility for their own destinies. American grassroots capitalism re-ignited. Creative minds that had been writing great songs all along now had opportunities to invent new markets and new methods of promotion. Their innovations did end-runs around the music establishment.

In 1999, the tremors turned cataclysmic when eighteen-year-old Shawn Fanning, a college dropout, created Napster and sprung the lock on Pandora's Box. Shawn's idea was the genius of the obvious. Like most teenagers, he and his friends liked to share and swap music. Shawn found a way to do it through a central Internet server. Kids (and their parents too) who were sick of paying $18 for a CD with only one or two good songs on it, were having the time of their lives finding and downloading songs they really liked using Napster—*for nothing*! Music moguls gasped and panicked. They broadcast public service announcements against file sharing and started suing kids who used the new technology. The original Napster was eventually shut down. But the barn door remained open. The horse was long gone.

So Is All This Progress Good Or Bad For Music...And For Me?

We have all heard the doomsayers' predictions: *Music will not survive the advent of Internet file sharing.* Record labels claim that illegal downloads have cost them billions of dollars in sales and have led to an industry-wide recession. Their complaint has a certain plausibility: *Why would people purchase recordings they can download for free?* Big labels and entertainment groups have filed lawsuits against thousands of end-users—most of them juveniles—caught stealing copyrighted material over the Internet. But corporate litigation against individuals is unlikely to make a significant dent in the volume of illegal file sharing. Statistics report more than a billion illegal downloads every month!

Amazing! Has Anything Like This Ever Happened Before?

This is certainly not the first time the music industry, as a whole, has foretold doom and gloom in the advent of new technology. Truth is, the Old Guard has a long history of throwing up its hands in despair whenever technological innovations threaten the status quo.

Take the radio, for example. The technology had been under development for many years when it first became commercially available in the 1920s. By the late 1930s it was both widely available and affordable for most homes. As it gained ground, the outcry in the industry grew shrill: *Radio listeners would have no incentive to purchase sheet music or phonograph records. The loss in sales would surely destroy the music business!* At first this dire prediction looked set to come true. Record and sheet music sales plummeted over ninety percent as Americans purchased radios for their homes and enjoyed easy access to the songs they loved.

Then, as now, forward-thinking artists saw that the new technology was here to stay—whether the record companies liked it or not. They realized they had a simple choice. They could either fight it, or embrace it and see where it would take them.

Duking It Out

The legendary artist Duke Ellington was one of those who saw the promise of radio. Ignoring cynics who said jazz could never be effectively broadcast over the radio, he began airing his band's performances from New York on a program called *Live from the Cotton Club*. The show was a huge hit! The national exposure it generated propelled Ellington to national prominence and gave him the credibility and freedom to compose some of his most brilliant works. Eventually, of course, radio became music's best friend—and it's still one of the most effective ways to introduce new artists to the masses.

Duke Ellington, like most music legends, understood that music and its creators will always find a way to flex, adapt and reinvent themselves. He instinctively understood that…

> *It's much more effective to be PRO-active than RE-active. It's much better to be "for" things than against them.*

The Sky Really Isn't Falling, Chicken Little

OK, back to the twenty-first century. Not a lot has changed except for technology.

Napster appeared in 1999, and soon thereafter CD sales plummeted—especially between 2000 and 2002. Reports of artists and writers robbed of their livelihood flooded the media, conjuring images of soup lines on skid row. A whole new generation of doomsday prophets began to point the finger at the latest culprit—Internet file sharing.

Beneath all the chaos—deep within the halls of academia—two economics professors began quietly studying the filesharing phenomenon, crunching facts and numbers. In March 2004, Dr. Koleman Strumpf from the University of North Carolina and Dr. Felix Oberholzer of Harvard Business School released their four-year study in a paper entitled *The Effect of File Sharing on Record Sales: An Empirical Analysis.*

Like master jewelers examining every facet of a diamond for flaws, Professors Strumpf and Oberholzer looked at CD sales and file sharing from every possible angle and made some stunning discoveries. I'm going to summarize their conclusions next, but if you are standing up (and especially if you believe the nay-sayers) you may want to sit down and take a few deep breaths before you read their findings.

Here we go…

After four years of intense study, the economists discovered to their total shock that illegal downloads had virtually no effect on CD sales! In fact, they were so surprised by what they found that they spent more than two years re-analyzing their data. Each time their conclusions were the same. The professors write:

> *We find that file sharing has only had a limited effect on record sales.... This estimated effect is statistically indistinguishable from zero despite a narrow standard error. The economic effect is also small. Even in the most pessimistic specification, five thousand downloads are needed to displace a single album sale.*[3]

That's right! It would take five thousand downloads to decrease the sale of a CD by one unit!

And the study went further. File sharing was not just relatively innocuous when it came to lost music revenue—it actually increased sales.

> *File sharing…has considerably increased the consumption of recorded*

music...[it] lowers the price and allows an apparently large pool of individuals to enjoy music. The sheer magnitude of this activity, the billions of tracks which are downloaded each year, suggests the added social welfare from file sharing is likely to be quite high.[4]

I had the privilege of visiting with Dr. Strumpf recently. As we chatted about his study and its amazing conclusions, he commented that file sharing has become a way for people to taste, sample and learn about different kinds of music they would never otherwise have heard. Individual preferences in music are becoming far more eclectic and people are buying more music in a wider panorama of styles.

Shop Till You Drop

Think of it this way...

You go into a department store—just to browse a little and see what's in for the new season. As you pass the artfully displayed clothing, a certain color or look catches your eye; a new style from a new designer. You don't know much about that particular clothing line and you've never owned anything from that company, but you're intrigued by what you see.

What do you do next? You start pulling out the clothes that catch your fancy and you head for the dressing room where you can try on all of them...for free! Some outfits you thought would look terrific don't do anything for you when you put them on. Other outfits that you never would have considered before make you look and feel amazing. You buy the ones you like. The store considers this a successful sale.

But suppose you had to purchase every article of clothing you took into the dressing room *before* you tried it on? I don't know about you, but I would be much less adventurous—choosing only those items I really needed and brands I was familiar with.

This is exactly the way people had to buy music before Internet file sharing became widespread. If you wanted a specific song, you had to purchase an entire album to get it. I can't tell you how many times I parted with $17 or $18 just to get "that one song". When I played the album, I found the other songs on it were awful. I never listened to them again. Accordingly, I became extremely cautious about the recordings I purchased—choosing only those by my favorite artists.

Then Napster appeared, re-introducing the concept of "the single" to a world of burned-out consumers like me. Although Napster was ultimately shut down and forced to re-organize, the paradigm had changed forever. Consumers were no longer willing to pay for stuff before they took it into the dressing room. They would try on new sounds and expand their musical tastes with impunity. And it's not that they wanted everything for free. They just wanted to purchase songs they liked at a reasonable price.

Geeks to the Rescue

It was a simple matter of supply and demand. Customers were demanding a change in the way they obtained their music. It was up to the music industry to create new and legal ways to supply them. Ironically, though, it was not the music business that read the signs of the times and responded. It was a computer company!

In 2001, Apple Computers released its newest sensation—the incredible iPod. Then in 2003, it launched iTunes Music Store where songs could be downloaded legally for 99 cents. Consumers responded in droves. They could now try on and purchase songs from genres previously unheard…from artists flying under the radar…even artists in other countries.

You might guess that the music industry had at last seen the light and was backing these sensational innovations. Hardly! In 2001 many music insiders hadn't even heard of Napster yet—let alone the iPod. I remember making a trip to Nashville in 2002 where I met with several major industry executives. When I mentioned the Napster Revolution, they seemed but vaguely interested, shrugged their shoulders, and then went back to talking about the latest insider Nashville production. It began to dawn on me that many major players in the business were completely out of touch with what was already happening all over the country. They were still doing business the old fashioned way—the way it was done twenty-five years ago. No wonder it wasn't working!

Steve Jobs, Apple's cool geeky genius CEO, had nearly the same experience I did when he first approached the major music companies to discuss the impact of the Internet on the future of music. In a 2003 interview with *Rolling Stone*, Jobs recalls being kicked out by the major companies for more than a year and a half before his persistence and accurate predictions finally won him a hearing with the mega labels.[5] They finally began to get it and have been playing a game of catch-up ever since.

Experimentation with singles on the Internet has led to sales—but not just by major record companies and artists. Independents are getting their shot too. Songs are still being delivered to consumers but in different ways than before. Music shoppers are becoming more adventurous but far more savvy. They want their money's worth. They want to purchase music they like. The single is back. Competition is healthy. The bar of excellence for songwriting has been raised. Things are changing.

MY TWO CENTS' WORTH

In my opinion, what is happening to music in the twenty-first century is not simply a matter of economics. It is cultural. Songs are intellectual property that can and should be a source of revenue for their creators, but music is not just another product. It is part of our lives, our cells, our souls.

As long as people have been singing, they have been "sharing files." They have gathered for hymns around pianos. They have strummed dulcimers and taught their children the plaintive songs of the hills. They have wailed spirituals in the cotton fields of the South. They have carried their songs westward with the wagon trains and northward on Mississippi riverboats. They have brought their melodies from every corner of the earth, funneling them through immigration lines at teeming ports of entry—blending them with the rhythms and cadences of other races and cultures to create music that is distinctly American. Files have been shared for generations on printed sheets, piano rolls, Victrolas, 78, 45 and 33 1/3 rpm phonograph records, cassettes, CDs—and now, they are shared electronically.

Songs are for sharing. They always will be. The Internet has simply changed the medium.

So What Does All This Mean To Me Here In Boondocks?

Changing trends are only worrisome to those who have always done it the old way. As an independent songwriter and artist you never had any stake in the old paradigm anyway. The truth is that you are ideally situated to take advantage of unprecedented opportunities and find your place in the brave new world of music.

Water Water Everywhere

Twenty-five years ago most people would have thought the idea of selling water in bottles insane! When we were thirsty we simply went to the faucet in our kitchens for a drink of water. Who would pay for what you could get for free?

Today we are complete water snobs. We buy bottled water by the cases. We have our favorite designer brands—Evian®, Propel®, Deja Blue®, Aquafina®… and the list goes on. Here is the question for us:

> *Did free access to tap water stop capitalists from creating a multi-million dollar bottled water industry? Of course not. Recent studies find that Americans drink both tap water and bottled water. Amazing!*

Cups of All Kinds

Let's change the analogy to coffee. Coffee is the first thought on nearly everyone's mind as they stumble out of bed to greet another workday. But there are many choices in coffee. You might make yourself a cup of instant if you are alone first thing in the morning (you know, just to get the old motor started). Or, you might fire up your Mr. Coffee® and drip a whole pot for you and your spouse. Maybe you'll grab a 75-cent cup at the convenience store as you fill up your car.

But do all those cheap coffee options prevent you from visiting your favorite designer coffee establishment later in the day? Probably not. Four and five dollar frappa...cappa...half caf...soy milk...with double whip cream concoctions are selling like hotcakes! (And, did you know that Starbucks is now one of the leading distributors of music as well?)

Like water, coffee and a host of other commodities, music is no longer a matter of *either/or* but of *both/and*. Copyright protection is of course indispensable and illegal file sharing infringes on this protection in some ways. I am not advocating for this unlawful practice. But denial and nostalgia for the way things used to be won't turn back the clock.

The question is this: *Rather than fighting the wave of progress, how may we ride it to the shore of success?* The tide is rising. Your career depends on your rising with it. This is not an option. You must stay abreast of major trends and learn to use them. There is no room for laziness. You can't wait for luck or for someone else to do it for you. You will have to learn skills you never wanted to learn...take new approaches...try...fail...try again. Find a way to use the new technology to accomplish your goals.

You can do it from right where you are in Boondocks!

Are You Saying That Boondocks Might Become A New Music City?

If, by the term *music city*, you mean a city with deep musical roots and traditions, there are many communities that qualify.

For several years I have participated in an annual music conference in New Orleans. Amid the steamy bayous, in this amazing port city, eighteenth and nineteenth century European music mingled with African-American and Latin influences to spawn sounds and styles we now can't dream of living without—the Blues, Jazz, Dixieland, Zydeco and their relatives, R&B and Rock and Roll. New Orleans has always been a world of music unto itself… elegant, sophisticated. Funny how as time passed and music became an industry, it seemed New Orleans no longer really qualified as a music capital. It took the worst natural disaster in American history to remind us: New Orleans' musical roots are too deep to be unearthed—even by a hurricane.

Or think about Memphis with its colorful background in Gospel and Blues….or Austin with its tradition of Folk, Tejano and Texas Country music…or Miami, where the vision of Gloria and Emilio Estefan has helped to make Latin music part of the American music tapestry.

The fact is that every community is a music community—and there are many places with even deeper and richer musical foundations than the Big Three. *Before you pack up and move to Nashville, LA or New York, get to know the music city where you live.*

A Great Example

I recently had a wonderful conversation with legendary singer-songwriter, Michael McDonald about this very thing. When I asked Michael for the best piece of advice he could give an aspiring songwriter, he answered without hesitation, "Get to know your own music community."

Michael pointed out that 1960s Detroit was not a city that anyone expected would become a music capital. Most people who migrated to Detroit in those days did so in hopes of employment with the auto industry—not the music industry.

It was in an automobile plant in this industrial city that a genius music idea was born. Motown Records founder, Berry Gordy, recalls his dream of a "hit factory" was shaped by his experience on the Lincoln-Mercury assembly line.[6] His dream allowed gifted musicians to find each other and make music together. The result was a creative community that changed the world of Pop music forever.

As it was in the days of Motown, so it is now. Capitalism and entrepreneurship are alive and well—even in the music business. Only now, we have the technology to make world-class recordings right in our own living rooms and the means to share them with the world.

This is a fantastic time to be alive and making music, whether you are an unknown aspiring songwriter or have been a fixture in the industry for decades. The changes we are seeing today may seem like exciting opportunities or terrifying threats—perhaps a little of both. But one thing is certain: if you choose to weather the storm, you are in for a hell of a ride. Make sure you have your seatbelt fastened!

REWIND...

~ The music landscape of the twenty-first century will bear little resemblance to the past.

~ Capitalism combined with artistic creativity is creating new music cities all over the world.

~ Computer and Internet technology are making opportunities out of obstacles.

[1] Bob Dylan, *The Times They Are a-Changin'* © 1963 by Warner Bros., Inc. Copyright renewed 1991 by Special Rider Music. All rights reserved. International copyright secured. Reprinted by permission.

[2] Hal David and Burt Bacharach, *Do You Know the Way to San Jose?* © 1967 by New Hidden Valley Music (ASCAP), administered by Warner/Chappell, Casa David (ASCAP). Reprinted by permission

[3] Dr. Koleman Strumpf, Dr. Felix Oberholzer, *The Effect of File Sharing on Record Sales: an Empirical Analysis,* © March 2004, p.3

[4] Ibid., p. 26

[5] Jeff Goodell, *Steve Jobs: The Rolling Stone Interview*, © Rolling Stone Magazine, December 3, 2003

[6] Berry Gordy, http://motownmuseum.com/mtmpages/perform.html

NOTES

8

Developing Your Unique Shtick

There is no way to adequately express the extent of the revolution or the speed with which it is sweeping the world of music. Every day new horizons open with challenges all their own. Things inconceivable just a few years ago have become commonplace. (Just consider the ubiquity of Apple's iPod that first debuted in November 2001). By the time you become aware of a new Internet resource or recording technology, it is already being replaced by something even more cutting-edge. As opportunities flourish, so does the competition.

Pick up the *Arts and Entertainment* section of any weekend newspaper or local city tabloid and you will find scores of aspiring artists and bands pe forming at venues all over town. Most of them are short-lived collaborations. The money they make gigging at bars and bookstores in town is frequently insufficient to sustain them for long. Bands break up. Artists burn out and move on to other careers—careers that put food on the table.

Question: *What's the difference between a pizza and a songwriter?* Answer: *A pizza can feed a family of four.*

Facing the Music

You as an aspiring singer, songwriter, or musician must ask yourself a tough question and be prepared to give a brutally honest answer. The answer to this question will help you develop a realistic plan to promote your music. Here's the question:

**Why would a listener choose
my CD or my concert performance over the
thousands of others available?**

I told you it was going to be a tough question. But it is one that demands an answer if you hope to succeed. If we are going to leave Dreamland and touch down in Reality, we have to realize that there are talented artists who are signed to major labels today whose CDs will never sell enough to break even. Where does that leave you?

Think about it: the artists and songwriters who have risen to the top have all found an edge…something unique that sets them apart and draws listeners to their music. It doesn't have to be something as original as, say, Karen Carpenter's one-in-a-million voice, or the unmistakable bawling of Joe Cocker, for it to work. The fact remains that you as an artist need to distinguish your efforts from the many other artists competing for attention in your genre. Take artists like James Taylor, John Mayer and Norah Jones—all of them singer-songwriters playing Adult Contemporary Pop music with a touch of Folk influence. Each of them rearticulates the sound of that genre in a novel way, just enough to stand out, be recognized and sell millions of records. Now, a step further…

**Allow me to make a rather bold statement:
Every individual has that special something.
It's just that so few ever find it.
It may lie deep beneath the surface in some
out-of-the-way place we wouldn't think
to look. We have to mine it like
hidden treasure. I call it developing
your unique shtick.**

What Kind Of Word Is "Shtick?"

The word *shtick* is really a Yiddish word that can mean a set of identifying characteristics. It is often used with reference to comedians who create a distinctive persona that sets them apart from others.

Johnny Carson's unique shtick included his classic pretend golf swing, his dapper appearance, and comedic roles as the bumbling magician, Carnac the Magnificent, and the dishonest salesman, Art Fern. Characters like Matt Foley who lived in a van down by the river, and Barney the Chippendale wannabe were two aspects of Chris Farley's totally hysterical shtick. Jon Stewart's shtick is political comedy. Jack Benny's included his squeaky violin, his miserliness and that famous blank look. But shticks are not unique to comedians. The pianist Liberace wore flamboyant costumes and always had a candelabrum on his grand piano. Ozzie Osbourne bit the heads off bats. You get the idea.

For our purposes I'm going to define the word *shtick* a little differently: your shtick is your total package—all the unique and imaginative attributes that make you, *you!* It is no mere gimmick. Think of it as the sum total of your personal assets. It's your one-of-a-kind presence and it draws people to you, opening a way to their hearts.

You have a unique set of styles and attributes that have evolved from your life experiences and musical background. You are a one-of-a-kind—like your fingerprint. No one has your voice, or appearance, or perspective on life. You are a composite of the specific and varied influences that have brought you to this point in your journey. You are a whole package of potential just waiting to find its place in history.

Did you really get what I wrote in that last paragraph? Or did you just skim over it? If you didn't, read it carefully. Read it again. Do you really believe it? Let me say it one more time:

> *I don't care who you are or where you come from. I don't care how old or how good looking you are. I don't care whether you have been successful in music or have never had any success at all. You are a unique, valuable, talented person with all the gifts you need to impact the world in a way no one else can. The key is to know yourself so well that you always lead with your strengths.*

I regularly meet songwriters and artists trying so hard to be like others in the industry that they never discover—let alone cultivate and exploit—the gifts that would set them apart from the crowd. *They never find their unique shtick!*

Can You Elaborate A Little? Give Me Some Examples?

Don't Discard Your Trump Card

I recently consulted with the father of an extremely talented fifteen-year-old artist who is attempting to break into Country music. This young lady is a 5'10" knockout with a beautiful voice. She also happens to have won numerous awards for Jazz dancing. A prospective manager recently told her father that to make it in Country music, his daughter would have to forget about Jazz dancing because the two art forms just don't mix.

I say this is nonsense! I mean…what a package! A Country artist who can also wow her audiences with a phenomenal Jazz dance! In fact, it just might be her ability to dance that sets this girl apart from the herd and opens a way for her to succeed.

There's no doubt that Barbra Streisand's voice alone would have made her a music icon. But then, we may never have been enriched by her acting and quirky sense of humor in movies like *Funny Girl and Meet the Fockers*; or by her genius as a composer in songs like the Academy Award-winning *Evergreen*; or by her screenwriting, directing and production skills in the multi-award winning movies, *Yentl* and *Prince of Tides*.

If Canadian Guy Laliberte´ had had to choose between fire breathing and his love of music, between acrobatics and choreography—we may never have witnessed the wonder of *Cirque du Soleil*. And had the multi-faceted Jamie Foxx been made to focus on just one of his many talents—if he had accepted that being a classically trained pianist just didn't mix with stand-up comedy or his desire to act, we might never have been graced by his Academy Award-winning role in the 2004 movie, *Ray*. It was Jamie's skill as a pianist that made it possible for him to learn from Ray Charles the intricacies of arrangement and performance that made the old jazzman a legend in his time.

The Luck of Liabilities

Comedian Josh Blue is an extremely funny guy. He is a recent winner of the hit TV series, *The Last Comic Standing*. Josh also happens to have cerebral palsy. But Josh has made a physical attribute that some consider a disadvantage the essence of his unique shtick. Cerebral palsy has provided him a unique range of perspectives and references that he is able to exploit for laughs, avoiding tired jokes and worn-out gimmicks. To his audiences Josh's insights are fresh and hilarious. Just being himself, Josh shows that it's OK not to take ourselves so seriously; that we don't have to be uncomfortable around people who are unlike us; and most importantly—that there is absolutely no such thing as a liability when it comes to finding your shtick. It's all in the way you look at what you have.

American Idol Triage

Last summer my colleague Sarah Marshall and I traveled to Austin to set up what we called an *American Idol Triage Center* outside the stadium where the Idol auditions were held. Our triage center was a park bench under a tree across the street. We offered cold drinks in the scorching summer heat, and an opportunity to practice (before the audition) or debrief (afterward) for the many talented young people who had come seeking their shot at fame. This was it. This was their big chance.

As you can imagine, many heartbroken people landed on our bench. When they came out of the auditions with a rejection, most concluded they just weren't good enough: they didn't have what it takes to be a star. They tended to focus on the ways their vocal performances had fallen short.

Sarah Marshall is a career consultant and life coach. Unique shticks are her specialty! I watched and listened as she began to talk with these young people. One beautiful young woman with a remarkable voice stands out in my memory. Sarah asked her a number of questions about herself, questions about other things she enjoyed doing—things besides singing—questions about her background, her family, her life experiences.

As she began answering these questions I had the distinct impression of watching a rose unfold. There was a good deal more to this artist than her voice! She had a wonderful interracial life history with many cultural and musical influences. She was a songwriter, a painter, a photographer and a computer graphics whiz. She had produced videos and scored films with her own music. Not long ago her father had passed away and she had gone through a difficult grieving process that deepened her compassion for others.

As Sarah visited with her, it became clear that this young artist had completely missed her shtick. She was competing on just one level—the vocal performance level. She was like someone with a whole suitcase full of outfits, who wears the same one every day.

As we discussed ways she could put her unique gifts and talents together, she began to get it:

> *Wherever it is you're headed and wherever you end up, be sure you get there running on all six cylinders.*

So How Do I Discover My Unique Shtick?

Refuse to be an Imitation

We all grow up admiring famous people. We are in awe of their talent. We envy their celebrity, their financial prosperity, and their glamorous lifestyles. We want to be just like them. We begin to walk in their footsteps. We try to sing, speak, dress and live as they do.

We see and hear our favorite artists on the radio and TV so frequently that it seems we know them. But remember, all we are really getting is a glossy media façade. As human beings, they are a good deal more and less than a highly manipulated image on the screen. If you compare the person you are on the inside with the bulletproof celebrity veneers you see and hear, you will find yourself at a disadvantage. Every time.

Clearly, the artists who dominate the media exert a powerful influence on the way we as songwriters and musicians create music. The songs we hear on the radio, television and online can be an important source of inspiration and new ideas. But not always. That's why it's so important to know and study the *great* hit writers. One hit wonders are a dime a dozen and much of what passes for cutting edge is little more than a tedious pantomime of the current trendsetter. An artist's moment in the limelight may be short lived but while it lasts she becomes the boilerplate for those legions of copycats and wannabes out there dreaming of making it big.

Every once in a while someone makes an original contribution, using familiar devices and techniques to reinvent the sound of a genre. She is typically the exception to the rule. The majority is content with uncritically mimicking its idols. Of course no one remembers the imitators. Time has a way of sifting them out.

Don't be a Shtick in the Mud

This is a crucial part of finding your unique shtick. You may start out with a specific goal or idea in mind, but if you hold to the original objective too rigidly, you may miss something far better than what you had planned.

Entertainment attorney Donald Passman, author of the best seller, *All You Need to Know About the Music Business*, recalls his early ambition to play guitar. Like almost every other red-blooded American boy, he dreamed of becoming a rock star. While playing in a band called *Oedipus*, he pitched a demo of the band's original songs to producer Snuff Garrett. Snuff's advice: "Don…go to law school."[1]

Don recalls:

> *…it was becoming apparent that my ability to be in the music business and eat regularly lay along the business path.*[2]

Don got involved in music because he loved playing it. He stayed because he discovered he was better at the business and legal aspects…and he was smart enough to face reality and lead with his strengths. He writes:

> *As I began to really understand how the music business worked, I found that my love of both creative arts and business allowed me to move smoothly between the two worlds and help them relate to each other. The marriage of art and commerce has always fascinated me, and the process of taking complex business concepts and cutting them into small, digestible chunks is a challenge I really love.*[3]

Donald allowed Snuff to steer him to where his unique gifts could flourish. We, who have read his book and have come to understand the music business a little better as a result, are grateful he did not insist on playing guitar for a living.

Music is a journey. It's a winding path along which you pick up a number of creative skills. Be interested in all aspects of it. Learn from the people whose paths cross yours. Listen to those who have walked the way before you.

> *Your destiny is somewhere no one else has ever gone. To discover it you will have to leave the familiar and traverse uncharted terrain. What you find may surprise you.*

Do a Searching and Fearless Inventory

I said earlier you would have to mine your unique shtick like buried treasure. Most people have never even scratched the surface. They hope on a star for the chance to trade it all in—their real lives for the pomp and glamour of becoming a music sensation. The fact is they have never left the comfort of who they wished they were in order to find out who they really are. And therein lies the difference. Between wanting to be someone you aren't and actually having something to say, there is a job of self-discovery to do. What it is you have to say and how you'll say it may require some excavation. So get your lantern and your pick ax and let's start.

Take a legal pad and divide the page into four columns:

In the first column list all the things you know you are good at.

> These are things you enjoy doing most—things you know you will do for the rest of your life whether you get paid for doing them or not. You probably enjoy things that come easily to you—activities that are in line with your gifts and strengths. Let your mind free flow. List everything you can think of.

> Don't disregard anything. If you are a talented skier, list it. Who knows? It may come in handy when you try to find a creative way to market your songs. Has anyone written and produced a CD to ski by?

> Compliments from other people can help you pick out your strengths. If you are a performing singer/songwriter, pay special attention to the songs that get the biggest responses from your audience. Try to figure out why your audience likes one song better than the rest. Is it an original song or a cover? Is it the arrangement? The subject matter? The melody? The guitar riff? The clever lyrics? Positive audience response is one of the best indicators of your unique talent. Write it all down in column one.

In the second column, list skills that are not quite strengths—ones you feel confident you can improve.

> If you are a beginning guitar player, for instance, list this in column two. You may not be concert quality yet, but with enough practice, you know

you could be pretty durn good. Add to this list activities that you don't particularly like to do now, but that you might learn to like if you were more skilled at doing them.

Kevin E. James is a country singer/songwriter who has been performing at venues throughout the Southwest for several years. He has a quick wit and a folksy sense of humor. And the stories he tells about his quirky family and upbringing in East Texas are a hoot! Give Kevin a few minutes reminiscing and he has his friends in stitches. But for some time Kevin was a little insecure about plying his brand of humor before a crowd. He was at ease as a singer, but not as a standup comedian.

So Kevin enrolled in a standup class taught by a professional comedy coach. He learned the fine points of timing and delivery. Soon he was performing at comedy clubs and adding a little standup routine to his already polished vocal performances. Developing this skill added a new dimension to Kevin's shows. It built an easy rapport with his audiences and drew a more enthusiastic response to his music.

In the third column, list all the things that you are lousy at.

There is a commonly held American can-do philosophy that says:

*You can do anything you want to if you
believe in yourself and set your mind to it.*

I would disagree. No matter how hard you try or how much you believe in yourself, there are some things you will not be able to master. You may be able to grasp the basics, but you'll never be an expert. It flat ain't gonna happen.

If your high school counselor calls you into his office (as mine did) and tells you that your verbal scores are in the 96th percentile but that your math skills are in the 34th…and if he then urges you *not* to attempt any kind of occupation that requires higher mathematics…then math falls into the third column. Although I can balance a checkbook and figure out which brand of green beans is the best value per ounce, I will never be a math whiz!

In the fourth column list any life experiences, physical difficulties or special challenges you believe are a roadblock to your dreams.

Perhaps you had a difficult—even abusive—childhood that has left you feeling wounded and insecure. Perhaps you have always believed you are physically unattractive (too short, too fat, too…something). You may have struggled with an eating disorder, an addiction or faced other challenges that have been difficult to overcome.

Drag those deficits out of the closet and list them—remembering there is no such thing as a liability when it comes to finding your unique shtick.

Now take a realistic look at yourself. Ask yourself the following questions:

♫ *Are there any assets in column one that might help me to promote my songs in a way that hasn't already been done by other artists or writers?*

♫ *Are there underdeveloped skills in column two that might be improved to enhance my column one talents? If so, just how do I improve? What practical steps can I take this week to begin mastering these skills?*

♫ *Do I know anybody with the skills I lack who might be willing to work with me?*

♫ *What physical, emotional or life difficulties have I experienced that I might use to my advantage if I were to look at them differently?*

♫ *Is my unique shtick coming into focus?*

But How Is All This Going To Help Me Make Money?

Good question. Turn to the next page on your legal pad. We're going to do some more writing, but before we start, let's look at a small word that can make the difference between life as a starving artist and cash money. The word is *niche*. It has several interesting meanings

1) The first (and probably the oldest of the meanings) is *a recess in a wall for holding a statue or an urn*. Keep that definition in mind as we go on to a second and more contemporary one.

2) *A situation or activity especially suited to a person's interests, abilities or nature*—as in "he has really found his niche in life."

3) The third definition is related to the second but goes a step further: *a special area of demand for a product or a service*. In other words, it's a vacuum clamoring to be filled…a question insisting on an answer. It's a gap in the impenetrable wall.

Now, let's put these three definitions together so they apply to you.

Have you ever had the feeling that trying to break into the music business is like beating your head against a stone wall? If not, you haven't been doing this long enough. I've got news for you…it's not just a feeling. The music business *is* a stone wall, almost impossible to penetrate, climb over, dig under or go around. But you can create a niche…a little hollow or recess in the wall that will hold you. It will be a place where you shine like a beautiful ornament against a monotonous backdrop. It will be a place uniquely suited to your interests, abilities and nature, and it will be a space that no one else can fill quite like you can.

Discovering Your Niche

Now, turn to a fresh page. List every way you can think of to sell your product from right where you are in Boondocks. Could you put your CDs on the counter in your sister's beauty salon? Could you sell them door-to-door? Could you do a concert at an assisted living center and sell CDs there? No matter how zany the idea, list it. These ideas will provide the raw material necessary to develop your creative marketing strategy later.

Now, sit down with your evaluation and take an objective look at yourself in the context of society as a whole and your community in particular. Like any other successful business, you must find a niche to fill…you must find something unique to bring to the table that brings consumers to *you!*

You may want to ask a friend who knows you and your community—and who has a creative perspective—to help you at this point.

Ask yourself:

♫ *What unmet needs or unserved audiences do I see in my community? (The key words in this question are "unmet" and "unserved"—they refer to opportunities that have not already been exploited by other singers or songwriters.)*

♫ *How might I combine my musical talents and other gifts to create a service or product that meets those needs?*

♫ *How might my unique shtick help to create an identity that sets me apart from other singer/songwriter/musicians?*

♫ *How do I develop an image that appeals to as many people as possible without compromising my artistic integrity?*

Answers to these questions will help you identify audiences and communities where your particular combination of aptitudes will be welcome and where you may also start making some money.

Fish in a Different Pond

As you already know, I am a huge fan of the local songwriters' group. It is a great way for artists and writers to get to know and network their own music communities. Be aware, however, of the inclination to "group think" within such organizations. Over a period of time members can come to think alike. We start to believe that success means imitating the successes of others by performing at the same venues, recycling the same tired styles and sounds. We begin stepping on each other's toes and the competition gets fierce. There are too many people trying to do the same things…in the same places…in the same ways.

Let me be very clear: songwriting organizations are terrific. But be on guard. Songwriters who spend too much time talking to other songwriters can easily begin thinking in less and less original ways about their music.

When we move out into the Internet songwriting community, the group think problem is exponentiated. Large Internet distributors of independent music cater to thousands of artists and writers at all levels of talent. Songwriting websites host forums and chat rooms that allow for the communication of tips and suggestions across a worldwide songwriting community. The sheer number of artists doing the same thing in the same places is overwhelming.

Let's return to the question we posed earlier:

**Why would a listener
choose my CD over the thousands of others
available to them?**

The answer to this question lies in identifying your unique shtick and finding a niche that has not already been filled. We're looking for ponds to fish in with lots of fish in them and very few fishermen.

How Am I Going To Find A Pond Like That?

Surplus Versus Service

Most songwriters and artists live for the day when they'll really start making some cash—hopefully lots of it—with the music they love to create. The more hard working and ambitious among us study marketing and promotions. We often spend a good deal of money trying to make more money. The key is to change direction—just about 180 degrees.

The secret of developing a successful shtick is this: Rather than trying to make a surplus, find a way to be of service.

As you continue networking within your music community, don't forget to look beyond the sometimes insular world of artists and musicians. Most consumers are not musicians. They are ordinary people who want music to help them through their day. Find those people. They will welcome and esteem your talent. You won't have to compete to be validated by them.

The hard won wisdom of my years in the music business is that when an artist focuses on making money, she almost invariably tends to do what everyone else is doing to make money. If your objective is to be of service to others, however, you will find ways your music can meet an unmet need… touch a hurting heart…light a child's eyes. In the process you will discover new audiences.

Songs of Love

So how many songwriters have written 10,000 hit songs? John Beltzer has. None of them have reached the top of the charts, but they are hits all the same.

Some years ago John was an aspiring singer/songwriter with dreams of becoming a star. Then something happened that changed the course of his life and music forever. In 1984, John saw his twin brother Julio commit suicide. In his grief he began searching for ways to use his music to serve others and honor Julio's memory. He remembered that his brother had once written a song called *Songs of Love*. Suddenly, he had an idea. He telephoned St. Jude's Children's Hospital in Memphis and asked for the names of six critically ill children. Within ten days he had written personalized songs for each of them. When one of the kids called to thank John for her song, he knew that he had found his calling.

Operating out of his New York City apartment, John founded the *Songs of Love Foundation* in 1996, the only non-profit organization of its kind. Seriously ill children, their parents and their health care providers are given personalized questionnaires that help them identify a child's favorite things—foods, pets, colors, games, people, styles of music, etc. One-of-a-kind compositions are written with song lyrics capturing happy images from each child's life. No two songs are the same. Many kids coping with life-threatening diseases have reported that their special songs brought them hope and healing—helping them endure painful treatments and lifting their spirits.

Over the past decade John's love songs project has enlisted the help of more than 300 talented artists and writers nationwide—including major artists like Michael Bolton, Nancy Sinatra and Billy Joel. Requests for songs pour into the foundation daily from hospitals and health care institutions the world over, but no matter how many songs are written, the goal of *Songs of Love* remains the same: to keep giving encouragement and love to those who need it most, using music as medicine.

Over the years John Beltzer's work has received a good deal of media coverage and won recognition for his music, but his real reward is seeing a smile light up the eyes of a suffering child. In his quest to serve, John discovered an entirely new audience. Life and music have led him to a singular success.

For more information on John Beltzer and to find out how you can be a part of Songs of Love, visit **www.SongsOfLove.org**.

From the Sewing Room to the Studio

Here's an example from my own life.

Several years ago I had come to a crossroads in my music career—a crossroads that, at the time, looked more like a dead end. We've all been there, right? You've achieved a measure of success, but then everything starts heading south. Money gets tight and good opportunities seem light years away. Such was my predicament.

There I was sitting in my office (which also doubled as my sewing room) listening to the phone *not* ring. I was depressed and just plain tired of the struggle. I began reviewing my "poor me list" of reasons for hanging it all up and going back to sewing. I didn't sing. I didn't live in Nashville. I had no money and few industry connections…the list went on!

But then something said, "You're know, you're right. You don't have any of these things. Now let's take a look at what you do have." I did a quick inventory just as described and looked hard at what I had and what I could do rather than what I didn't and couldn't. As you can well imagine, in my depressed frame of mind my debits far outweighed my credits, but I did have health…I knew how to write songs (albeit songs no one was hearing)…and I loved working with people. But where would that take me?

Just then I spotted a box on top of my bookshelf. It was overflowing with tapes from aspiring songwriters. My small publishing company had been listed in the *Songwriter's Market Book* that year (Writers Digest Publishers). Mine was just one among thousands of classified ads, but it had resulted in a large number of submissions.

It dawned on me that the one thing I had plenty of was material from other songwriters who were trying to overcome the same obstacles I was facing. Here was an obvious need—songwriters desperate for help polishing and promoting their songs! What did I have that might fill that need? I had health…I knew how to write songs…and I loved working with people! I had been asked to do some songwriting seminars and had really enjoyed teaching. Hey…maybe this was the connection!

To make a long story a little longer, an idea was born in that moment in my sewing room that resulted in the creation of my radio talk show for aspiring songwriters, *I Write the Songs.* As I continued to explore my unique shtick and let my creative juices flow, I began to realize that what some might call a niche—the community of aspiring songwriters—was really a huge market of more than 50 million people.

To be sure, there was a lot to learn about radio. I spent weeks and months in the learning curve and was often stretched, but I was doing something that I really enjoyed and I was exercising my gifts.

It has been an amazing journey from the sewing room to the studio, and one that I never imagined would result in the experiences and fun I have had. And the beat goes on as I am now writing my first book—and you're actually reading it! Who woulda thunk?

I have the privilege of meeting aspiring writers all over the country—and around the world thanks to the Internet. I love seeing talented people grow and blossom and when I help others avoid the potholes I hit, I feel as if the lessons I learned in the School of Hard Knocks have been worth it.

I have visited with some of the most famous songwriters in the world—people I never dreamed I would ever meet in person. One thing I have discovered is that all of us flaky tunesmiths love talking about our songs and hearing our fellows talk about theirs. I stumbled into a niche that was right under my nose…sitting right there in a box on my shelf, a niche of millions of people who want the talents I can bring to the table, a niche that fits perfectly with my unique shtick.

To hear the radio show I Write the Songs, visit **www.IWriteTheSongs.com**.

So How Do I Try Out My Unique Shtick?

Early in my career I was shocked to discover that as an industry, the music business is among the *least* creative in the world. Going into it I thought I would find innovative, out-of-the-box thinkers all over the place. Instead, I found *Group Think, Inc.*

Rather than searching for new concepts in music, most industry execs are watching their competitors to see what is earning *them* money. Their strategy is almost invariably to go and do likewise. That's why when one label finally signs a successful child artist (as Curb Music did with LeAnn Rimes) you then have a whole series of younger and younger artists signed by competing labels—labels which, pre-LeAnn, were dead set against the legal risks involved in signing kids.

You, as an independent artist/songwriter, have the privilege of thinking more creatively, of innovating in ways the industry never will. You don't have to get an idea approved by some suit in a record company office before you try it. Go ahead. Experiment with creative ideas for funding and promoting your demos and recordings. If what you try doesn't work, quit. Just go on to something else.

As songwriter Steve Gillette once told me:

> *The independent musician is kind of like a schooner. He can go anywhere an ocean liner can, but he can make sharper turns.*

Cowboy Creativity

Consider the case of David Cline, a business owner, cowboy, rancher and truck driver with a wonderful baritone voice. He's also a darn good songwriter. But David is fifty-plus, well beyond the age limit for new artists hunting record deals. He lives in Texas where some of the greatest music in all genres originates, but a place that until recently, has been little regarded as a music capital. Several years ago, David decided to record a CD of Cowboy and Traditional Country music, but found he had neither the money he needed to complete the project nor the connections to finance it.

But like many of us David is an out-of-the-box thinker. Capitalizing on his unique shtick as a rancher/cowboy/truck driver/singer-songwriter, he approached each of the retailers whose products and services he used in his day gig—saddle manufacturers, feed stores, cowboy hat and clothing merchants, truck stops, etc.—and asked them if they would like to sponsor his recording and music video. In exchange for a donation, he would credit them on the CD insert and include their products in his video.

The retailers were amenable and David was able to fund his recording. Later they were delighted to sell his CDs in their stores. Because of the exposure, he began receiving radio play and his songs charted in several Texas cities as well as on XM Radio and other Internet radio stations.

Instead of buying expensive advertising in music magazines, David sent his CD to niche consumer publications that would review it…trucker, trail riding, and RV magazines. Several gave him enthusiastic reviews. Sales began to mount.

Next, David started performing at a large local flea market in Canton, TX. The *First Monday* in Canton is a local attraction that draws thousands of people. David performed his Traditional Country songs as shoppers perused the many stalls. Flea market shoppers have cash, they love Country music and they bought David's CDs.

Through a contact in Canton, David learned about an even larger event in Quartzsite, AZ. Every year thousands of people bring their RV's to this beautiful spot to enjoy the rock formations. Vendors bring wares and stands sell everything imaginable. David and his wife, Becky, brought their RV and his sound system and soon he was selling CD's in Quartzite. (See what I mean about niches?)

Then David did some research and discovered a reputable independent promotions company that creates compilation CDs for distribution to foreign radio stations. Compilation CDs are recordings containing songs by several different artists that are distributed by promoters to radio stations for airplay.

Several months later, David learned that he was one of the most frequently requested independent country artists in several European markets. His CDs sold like hotcakes, and he was soon off to Europe for a seven-nation tour. Two years later the same promoter sent the compilation to New Zealand and before long David was on a plane heading way, way south. While he had to pay his own airfare, the CD sales and performances proved so lucrative that he realized a substantial profit.

You owe it to yourself to check out the story of David Cline and his amazing music career at **www.DavidCline.com**. Especially browse the reviews he has generated. He is the poster child for discovering and staying true to your unique shtick.

> *Bear in mind that like so many other service*
> *providers in this business, promoters come in*
> *all shapes and degrees of integrity. The key is to*

find a reputable one. There are many shysters who will eagerly take your money and include your song on a compilation CD. But then, you will never hear from them again. Be sure to research...research...research before you spend your hard-earned dollars and be sure that the promotion company sends you regular tracking records telling you where your song has been sent and what kind of response it is receiving.

Don't Overlook Little Shticks

We said at the beginning of this chapter that the Yiddish word *shtick* means identifying characteristic. Your talents may largely define who you are as a songwriter/artist, but give some thought to the ways simple innovations might dramatically enhance your persona.

For several years I have watched the emergence of a talented singer-song-writer from Texas. She is young, beautiful and has a wonderful voice. Unfortunately this is not enough to set her apart from the many other young, beautiful and vocally talented artists striving for success.

The last time I saw her perform I noticed that she had something in her hand as she took the stage. After the first verse and chorus of her song—she put a harmonica to her lips and blew a killer solo during the musical bridge. Wow! How cool! Now we have a young, beautiful, talented female singer who has an identifying talent—something a little different for a female artist. Now people say, "She's that girl with the harmonica!" Just a little shtick...but it might be enough to nudge her into the limelight.

Sometimes these little innovations just evolve. We don't plan them. They may occur spontaneously as when a band practices together and members develop a signature harmony, an instrumental technique and a stage presence. A solo performer may accidentally discover a couple of dance moves that galvanize his audience. It's chemistry. Serendipity. Don't just have fun with it. Be aware of what's happening. Look for it. Capture it. Use it to the max. It's all part of your package.

What If I Need Some Help with All of This?

As mentioned earlier, it is often helpful to have an objective party evaluate your progress. Sarah Marshall (mentioned earlier as giving triage to *American Idol* contestants in Austin) is especially gifted in this kind of work. As a career strategist, Sarah's gift is that of evaluating skills and designing creative new ways to maximize career opportunities.

For more information on Sarah Marshall Consulting visit:
www.FromNowhereWithNothing.com.

REWIND...

~ Your shtick is your total package...all the attributes that make you unique.

~ Maximizing your ultimate potential requires that you identify all your talents and skills—not just one or two—and that you lead with your assets.

~ When you have identified your unique shtick, find a niche—a need in your community or an unserved audience—where you fit and can make a contribution.

~ Let life and music guide you to your destiny rather than rigidly forcing the matter.

~ Be aware of little shticks—identifying characteristics that evolve as you do. Use them well.

~ Be on guard against "group think" wherever you may find it—in your community, on the Internet, or within the music industry.

[1] Donald S. Passman, *All You Need to Know About the Music Business*, p. 22, ©1991, 1994, 1997, 2000. Reprinted by permission of Simon & Schuster Adult Publishing Group.

[2] *Ibid.*

[3] *Ibid.*

NOTES

9

Growing Into Business

OK! I need a show of hands here! How many of you aspiring songwriters have ever heard or read something that goes kinda like this:

> *If you want to prove that you are really, really, really serious about making it in the music business, the first thing you have to do is sell your house, pack your stuff in a U-Haul, and relocate to LA, New York or Nashville.*

The wisdom behind this advice is clear—and it has proven successful for many now-famous songwriters. We touched on the rationale of this philosophy in chapter seven:

> *If you live in or near a major music capital, you will have access to many music-related opportunities that will not only help you to learn the craft and business of songwriting, but will put you in touch with industry insiders, who can help you "get a deal" (meaning a songwriter's agreement, recording contract or staff songwriter position).*

Since I first entered the music business over two decades ago, I have heard the *Move-to-Nashville-NYC-LA* advice over and over and over again. It has become a dogma of success for songwriters—one that separates the seriously motivated from dabblers. If a songwriter were unwilling to pick up stakes and move to a major music city, it proved she would never have the chops to make it. For me, the only problem was that moving just didn't make sense. I was a housewife with four kids in school. My husband had a career and we owned a home—in Texas!

Now, Texas is known for lots of things—wide open spaces, great Tex-Mex, longhorns, barbecue, cowboys and oil—but until recently (when it has begun to emerge as the Third Coast in music) it has not been considered a music capital. And as you know, Texas is smack dab in the middle of the country—nowhere near any of the traditional music cities. I quickly realized that if success as a songwriter depended on my moving to LA, New York or Nashville...it flat wasn't going to happen! I was willing to work hard and expand my knowledge of the craft and business of songwriting. I was motivated to do whatever it took to excel as a writer. But I simply couldn't uproot all the important people in my life to pursue an elusive dream. We had a wonderful life and home in Texas. I just couldn't see leaving everything behind to become one of thousands of other would-be songwriters waiting tables in a big music city in hopes that someone might discover me.

I would have to find alternative routes to my music goals. Since I didn't have a publisher or other inside connections to create opportunities for me, I learned to create them myself. This involved simple trial and error...and much dogged perseverance. It was a learning curve that led me into uncharted territory. Each day became a pilgrimage into new ideas and experiences. *Necessity truly is the Mother of Invention!*

Looking back over more than twenty years, it amazes me to see where I have been. I would never have met so many fascinating people nor had the adventures I did, if I had taken a more conventional path. And I am ever so grateful for the lessons I never really wanted to learn. They have only added to my love of music.

The point I am making here is that while moving to a major music city may be the ticket to success for some, it is no longer the only way to achieve your goals. If you are young, footloose and fancy-free and don't mind living on a shoestring while you follow your dream, you may very well decide to relocate. But, if like me, you have commitments and a career somewhere else, you will need to become an even better and more creative promoter than most music industry insiders.

Where Do I Start?

How about where you are with what you have? I call this *growing into business* instead of *going into business*.

The *going into business* approach dominates many new business ventures. You develop an idea for a new product or service. You raise venture capital, borrowing money and attracting investors. This gets you an office, a phone, a computer and—for musicians, of course—an instrument and recording equipment. It may even get you a ticket to New York, LA or Nashville. The fact remains that by the time your startup money runs out, your venture better have started up or you will join the ranks of great ideas that fizzled.

The other approach is to *grow into business*. It's not as exciting and glamorous on the front end, but it is far less risky and may lead to real longevity and ultimate success.

What Exactly Do You Mean by Growing into Business?

Crucial Credibility

Credibility is a very interesting word. In essence, it means to be trustworthy, believable. It has to do with how you are perceived by your listeners and by other members of the music community. Do others believe that you really know your stuff?

If you are an aspiring songwriter living in Boondocks, Montana, with no contacts at all in the music industry, you have to face the fact that you have absolutely no credibility when it comes to record labels and artists in far off music cities. They have never heard of you and have never heard your songs. No matter how good a writer you are, you're still a complete unknown.

If, however, you have a career and a social life and are not a convicted felon, you probably do have a lot of credibility in Boondocks. People know you and you know people. You know your way around town, where to shop, and the best places to eat. You have history in Boondocks it has taken years to build. This can be an amazing advantage to you as you extend yourself creatively.

Whether you are aware of it or not, there is wonderful talent right where you are. You may well find a whole network of gifted songwriters, musicians, lyricists, producers, composers and conductors without leaving your zip code. There may be some right there in your own neighborhood. If your day-gig is not music-related, you may not be aware of artists and musicians living on your block or even next door. (Would you believe that the songwriter who wrote *I Want My Babyback Ribs* for Chili's restaurants lives less than a mile from me?)

> *To grow into business as the promoter of your own songs, your first objective must be to locate and get to know other members of your music community.*

Is there an echo in here? We've been saying the same thing for nine chapters now. But repetition makes songs memorable. It might work the same way for one of the big themes of this book, right? So here we go again…this time with an illustration…

Look Around the Room

Several years ago I attended a large event for the Dallas area music industry, organized by NARAS (National Academy of Recording Arts and Sciences—the group that hosts the Grammys every year). As part of the evening program, a panel of industry professionals shared strategies for getting to the next rung on the music industry ladder. I found myself yawning a bit as several panelists gave the same-old-same-old relocation spiel I had been hearing for many years.

Then panelist Mathew Knowles, father of superstar Beyonce, addressed the crowd. In the sonorous voice of a preacher he asked all the songwriters in the room to stand. Several dozen responded. "How many publishers do we have in here?" he called. Several more rose. "How many entertainment lawyers…managers…producers…performing artists?" With each question his tone became more urgent. With each question more people stood up.

With nearly the entire room on its feet Knowles smashed his message home. "Now, look around the room," he said. "This is where your success lies. If you don't know every person standing, *you have no business moving anywhere!"*

Point taken! (We'll have more to say about Mathew Knowles and his sensational growing into business story in chapter eleven).

Look Around YOUR Room

What about you? Are you putting all this together? Just to be safe, let's hit that chorus one more time…

Watch your local paper for concerts, recitals, musical theater performances and other events. Join your local songwriters' association. Visit college and university music departments. Check out music programs and facilities in large or growing churches. Become familiar with names that keep popping up in music circles. Especially take note of up-and-coming singers who may be looking for original material. You will be astounded at the resources and opportunities right under your nose.

Now, make it your mission to introduce yourself to these people and get to know them. Pitch your songs to aspiring artists. Become an "insider" right where you live. Get acquainted with recording studios, engineers and producers. Let the music community know that although you are a professional in another field—a real estate agent, doctor, mechanic, accountant, contractor, or attorney—you are also a serious and skilled songwriter. Your name may ring a bell with those you meet. If they know you through your day job, you can begin trading on that credibility alone. These music types will perhaps be intrigued that you are also an accomplished songwriter.

> *Remember: You have far more credibility in the town where you live than you do in a distant music city. You also have immediate access to music people in your own community. Become a well-known and vital part of that group.*

With each acquaintance you make…with every new song you write or co-write…with every new music project you undertake, you are gaining credibility. In time, this credibility will begin to overflow your local area into wider and wider circles of influence.

The Strength of Survival

The best way to build credibility—both locally and nationally—is simply to survive! Nowhere in the world are there more here-today-gone-tomorrow stories than in the music industry. Someone has a hit song…or a great idea … and they appear to be the hottest thing on wheels. Then they vanish. Yesterday's sensations are rapidly replaced by newer, hotter acts. The public attention span is so short and fame is so fleeting we hardly pause to wonder where they went. You may never hear of them again. Then sometimes, lo and behold, they turn up years down the line on an episode of *Where Are They Now?* What happened? If they had the talent to create one hit, why didn't they have more successes? The answer is usually very simple. Somewhere along the line they got distracted or disillusioned…and they just gave up.

Contrast *you*—the aspiring songwriter. You may not have had a number one chart topper yet, but you consistently keep creating better and better tunes. You may be chewed up and spit out by the industry, but instead of giving up, you keep on keeping on.

You fight through your depression and you keep studying your craft, writing new songs, re-writing…and re-writing…and re-writing again. You keep turning out demos that improve with each production. Your songs start appearing on recordings by independent artists in your city or state and are performed in local music events. You are invited to speak at songwriters meetings. You keep hanging in there—even when you are just hanging on by a thread. All this builds credibility. The music industry may be changing, but you practice your craft with consistency and excellence. You are tenacious in your efforts to stay in touch. Believe me, the word will get out!

Eliminate the Word "Quit"

It has been said the most difficult word in the English language is *continue*. Every new enterprise is fun and exciting in the beginning, but when days turn into months…and years…those thrilling beginnings must evolve into an uncompromising resolve and the most relentless persistence if you hope to earn respect as a music professional. Keep suiting up and showing up year after year and—believe it or not—people will begin to assume that you know what you're doing (even if you're not always so sure yourself).

Think of it as equity. It's always fun to purchase or build a new home and to experience the anticipation of moving in and getting settled. But if you don't keep making those house payments month after month, the mortgage company will eventually foreclose and you will be out on your ear! No matter how difficult it may be to write those monthly checks, you do it because you know you must in order to achieve your dream. With each payment you own more house and owe less money. You are paying your dues and paying down the interest. You are building equity.

Remember: There is only one way to fail—and that's to quit. Don't quit! Your credibility depends on your survival.

So How Am I Going To Afford All This Growing Into Business?

Dollars and Sense

There are two ways to buy a white polo shirt. You can go down to Nordstrom's, find one you like and pay for it without checking the price tag. Or, you can shop around for the best deal.

As the mother of four kids on a limited income, I have always had to be very cost conscious. Savvy housewives learn early in the game that you don't always have to pay top dollar for the best quality. Not long ago a national television program aired a show on *How to Find the Most Value for the Least Money*. Consumer testing groups analyzed the quality and durability of several white polo shirts in different price ranges from various major manufacturers—Ralph Lauren, Tommy Hilfiger, Calvin Klein and several others. Guess which polo shirt won the contest for best quality—the seven-dollar shirt from Target!

In the last analysis, a white polo shirt is a white polo shirt, apart from the price tag you'll remove before you wear it (hopefully). No one will ever know whether you are wearing an expensive shirt or a cheap one. They *will* notice how well the shirt fits and how it looks on *you!*

So What Do Polo Shirts Have To Do With Growing A Music Career?

Plenty.

Just as you need to be aware of price and quality when considering polo shirts, you must learn to shop the good deals in recording, manufacturing and promoting your music. We touched on this subject when we examined the demo process in chapter three. If you are savvy and creative, you'll find inventive ways to produce the same quality recordings that major labels are releasing—only you'll do it with much less money.

I highly recommend that every aspiring songwriter or musician become involved in the process of recording, manufacturing and promoting a CD. You may decide to record your own or help with someone else's. Either way, it is an invaluable experience.

Learn to shop. Compare prices on everything. Watch for special offers. Ask lots of questions. Network…network…network. Learn every stage of the process. You will discover what the real costs are and you will know when you are being taken to the cleaners.

But If I Get A Record Deal, I Won't Have To Worry About All These Costs, Right?

Wrong!

Aspiring musicians are rarely so naïve as they are when signing that much-coveted record contract. The road to music stardom is littered with the carcasses of artists who accepted major label record deals on the mistaken assumption that at last their financial worries were over—only to find themselves some months or years later in massive debt and on the verge of bankruptcy. How does this happen?

When an artist signs with a major label, the label usually advances that artist a fixed amount of money to do a recording. The budget can range between $50,000 and $250,000 depending on the artist and her perceived potential. An artist sees this incredible sum and assumes that she may spend it freely without realizing what the word—*advance*—really means. You will remember this vocabulary word from chapter five when we discussed the songwriter's agreement and what it means to be a staff songwriter. An advance is not to be confused with a salary or payment. *It is a loan the record label intends to recoup from the royalties you earn.*

Recoup is another extremely important vocabulary word. It means payback on the advances. Tuck this word into your "rememberer" because we're coming back to it in just a minute. But first let's learn another word. In recording circles, royalties are often referred to as *points*. This is shorthand for percentage points based on the retail price of each CD sold. Fifteen points is, for example, another way of indicating 15 percent of the retail price of the record.

When an artist signs a record deal, the number of points making up the artist royalty is one of the key negotiation issues. The rate can vary, but usually ranges between 10 and 15 points. Often the artist never sees the first dollar of her artist royalty because until the production budget of the CD is recouped, all the artist's income goes to the record company. Additionally, the artist royalty rate may be designated an *all-in rate*. This means that if anybody else involved in the production of the CD is going to be receiving points or percentages (like a producer who may demand two…three…four points or more as part of her fee), those points are to be deducted from the artist's 10 to 15 point share.

In essence, singer-songwriters are required to recoup the costs for their own albums out of the 10 to 15 percent they are receiving in royalties. If the album doesn't recoup its production costs, the artist may never see the first penny of personal income.

This Can't Be As Bad As It Sounds… Can It?

Hey, we're just getting started.

Many major record contracts only pay artist royalties on 85 percent of the albums sold—a deduction taken for possible "breakage" during shipment. Royalty rates are also reduced for foreign sales and record club sales. Then there is the "free goods deduction," which says that there are two records shipped free for every ten that are purchased by a retailer. You guessed it…the artist is only paid royalties on the ten that are paid for. And on top of all this, there is the "packaging deduction." Labels can deduct up to 25 percent for packaging costs—far more than the real cost of packaging.

Are you starting to get the picture? Most new artists think their ship has come in when the label begins to advance them sizable monies for wardrobe, makeup, travel, tour support and video production. Months later, these same new artists get a statement from the label informing them what the word *recoup* really means. In short, it means the label ain't paying for squat! And at the end of the day, when the artist has reimbursed the label for all expenses, guess who owns the master recordings of the CD and probably the publisher's share of the original songs. The record company and its publishing arm...not the artist!

I'm afraid Hunter S. Thompson's celebrated quip comes dishearteningly so close to the truth:

> *The music business is a cruel and shallow money trench, a long plastic hallway where pimps and thieves run free and good men die like dogs. There's also a negative side.*[1]

Anybody Want To Give A Word Of Testimony?

Wy...Yes!

Wynonna Judd is one of my "she-roes." In addition to her amazing vocal and musical talents, Wy has always seemed to connect with her fans in a transparent way. She is what she is, and her vulnerable honesty makes her one of us.

In her riveting memoir, *Coming Home to Myself,* Wynonna writes candidly about her own business naiveté and how it almost drove her into bankruptcy, even after a mega-successful 20-year career.

She was only eighteen when she and her mother, Naomi, signed their first recording contract and were given the chance to bring their incredible musical talent to the world as *The Judds*. The excitement was electrifying. Wynonna was catapulted from a struggling hopeful to a household-name sensation—literally overnight. The signing of the contract was quickly followed by studio sessions, tours of the country, interviews, appearances, hair and makeup sessions, award shows and all the other trappings of stardom.

But like so many young artists, Wynonna didn't realize until many years later, when she had become a solo artist, that *she* (not the record label) was paying for everything—from recording costs to travel expenses, from sound equipment at concerts to costuming, hair and makeup. She had failed to grasp the full implication of the word, "recoup": *All the money advanced by the label had to be paid back before she made the first dollar.*

Toni's Story

Singer, Toni Braxton, has a similar story. She too surfed the music business tidal wave: a dizzying rise from anonymity to the heights of fame followed by a humiliating descent. From college student…to superstar…to Chapter Seven bankruptcy.

Her career began in 1992 when, as a university student aspiring to become a teacher, Toni was discovered by L.A. Reid and Babyface and signed to the new LaFace record label. Less than five years later she had become a major national artist selling more than fifteen million copies of her first two CDs.

But by 1998—just six years after signing her deal—she was filing for Chapter Seven bankruptcy protection with a reported debt of over three million dollars. All of her personal possessions were sold to pay her bills—including her five Grammys. What the heck happened?

Braxton later confessed that, like most people, she simply didn't understand the financial aspects of the business. She admitted that much of her own money was invested in the tours. She learned the hard way that everything—from the band…to the air travel…to the costume design—is paid for by the artist. If anything is left after all those advances have been recouped, the artist lives on that.

Thankfully Toni's story has a happy ending, due largely to savvy entertainment attorneys who helped her recover most of her possessions (including her awards) and negotiate a new and much better contract. During the ordeal Toni grasped the crucial point we have been making throughout this book: *Whether you are just starting out or have already sold millions of records, the responsibility for your career is yours and yours alone.*

So Are You Saying That All Record Deals Are Bad News?

Not at all.

To be fair, we have to acknowledge that record labels are taking a huge financial risk when they sign and fund an unproven artist or act. Would it shock you to learn that most artists on record labels sell less than five thousand units of their recordings?

When the label signs a new artist, it is gambling on the slim chance that this new act will be one of the few that actually makes money for the company. The record label acts as a venture capitalist in the music business—finding and funding what it believes will be revenue generating hit material at some time in the future. If an act becomes a true success—selling millions of albums and selling out dozens of concert venues—lots of money can and will be made by both the label and the artist. But it is usually only after blockbuster success that serious money begins to roll into the artist's bank account.

> *The point I want you to see is that the likelihood of mad financial success with a major label deal may be slimmer than a snowball's chance in you-know-where.*

So What Does All This Mean For Me Here In Boondocks?

Ok. Now let's contrast the fate of *you*—the independent songwriter/artist—growing into business and blooming where you are planted right there in Boondocks.

If you have done your homework and learned to shop at Target, you will be creating high fidelity recordings that sound as good as those of major labels—but at a fraction of the cost. You will have discovered the best values in recording studios, producers, engineers, graphic designers, printers and manufacturers. Major labels may advance their artists a recording budget of $50,000 or more, but you have learned to produce commensurate recordings for as little as $15,000 (sometimes even less). And since the only person you have to repay is *yourself*, you recoup your expenses at 100 percent instead of 10 to 15 percent. If you sell your CDs for $15, you will have covered your out-of-pocket recording expenses with the first 1,000 sold. Not only that, but you now own your masters—and are still your own DIY publisher!

After you have recouped your expenses, you will wisely designate a portion of the income from your CD sales for your next project. Soon you will have several CDs for sale at your concerts. They will be available through any local and national distribution outlets you have discovered. Even when you are selling your CDs wholesale to a store or distributor for 50 percent of retail, you are still making 50 percent. This level of recuperation is unheard of under the terms of a standard issue record contract. When you start crunching numbers, you quickly realize that you don't have to sell millions of records to break even. You can begin turning a profit with just a few thousand, and you are still in control of your creative output and the direction of your music career. Such a deal!

Some time ago I interviewed an exceptional artist who is making a wonderful living as an independent. She is such a marvelous talent that I had to ask her if she had ever been offered a major label contract. Her answer was that she had been offered several record deals, but in her words: "No one has ever been able to do for me what I can do for me." More and more artists are finding this to be true.

As you grow into business you will develop a dollars-and-sense understanding of the process that makes you far less vulnerable than the many who go into business only to find they have lost their music equity to the greed of the industry. Use your common sense and listen to your gut...and by all means, read the fine print in any negotiation with a knowledgeable music attorney!

So How Will Becoming A Success In Boondocks Ultimately Help Me Achieve My Dreams?

One of the most important principles I ever learned as a songwriter is this:

> *In the end, the music industry is far less interested in discovering new talent than it is in discovering proven successes.*

The hard reality is that the music business is first and foremost profit driven. In fact, it is one of the most lucrative industries in the world. The most important question for any music company is whether or not a prospective artist can turn a profit. Most savvy music moguls want to invest in artists and writers with proven track records and profit margins.

Here's a little parable that illustrates this important point:

Belinda and Betty are sisters. They both love to bake and they are both very good at it. Betty is probably a bit more creative. She not only bakes the traditional recipes for white, wheat and rye bread—she invents incredible new recipes that are always delicious. Belinda is not quite as gifted, but she works very hard, learning more about baking every day. Betty and Belinda's families love their fresh homemade bread, but so do other people in the community. The sisters have each been approached by friends and neighbors offering to buy their bread regularly. They are persuaded that they could make a real career out of baking, but here is where the two differ.

Belinda finds a small storefront shop that she can rent cheap. She fixes it up really cute and begins to sell her bread and muffins to the community. She doesn't have as many new varieties of bread as her sister, Betty, but the recipes Belinda bakes are great! As word spreads about her won-

derful bread, more and more people begin to buy Belinda's baked goods. Soon she has to hire an assistant baker…and then two. After a year she is able to buy a delivery truck to take her bread to the customers fresh and hot from the oven. Belinda now has enough money to expand her shop and add a couple more employees.

Betty, on the other hand, is so emotionally invested in her bread…she has poured so much of her heart and soul into creating each loaf…that she doesn't think of them as products. They are expressions of her gift as a baker. Betty doesn't feel it is necessary to open a bakery. She is sure that if she just keeps baking long enough, and inventing great new recipes— somehow, some way—she will be discovered by someone who will have enough money to open a bakery for her and pay her to keep on baking.

Here's the question...

If you were an investor looking for an opportunity to make money in the baking business, would you invest in Betty, the extremely talented baker—or would you be more inclined to invest in Belinda who may not be quite as gifted, but has the business savvy, creativity and discipline to find ways to sell her product to the world? Would you invest in talent alone…or in talent coupled with proven success?

Are You Saying That Talent Isn't Important?

Please don't misunderstand me.

Some actual talent is indispensable! You must stretch and exercise it daily. Hone it with every song you write. But talent is only the first rung in the ladder to the top and there are many other people standing on that same rung. Your mission—should you choose to accept it—is to find a way to take your talent to the next rung…and the next. Like any other business, the music industry is interested in beating the competition and making money. Believe me, record moguls and investors with an eye on the bottom line want to meet artists and writers who are already demonstrating success right where they are.

How Do I Present Myself As Successful?

I would suggest that you begin building a Success Resume today. Just as a business resume lists your education and business experiences, a Success Resume lists experiences and successes in your music career. Start now where you are, with what little you have, but get moving. Look for opportunities around you to show off your musical talent and as success, press coverage or fan mail begins to come your way, *keep a record of it all!*

What Exactly Is The Purpose Of A Success Resume?

Contrary to what you might think, a Success Resume is not just something you compile to feed your ego or get you out of a funk when you're depressed. A business resume details your experience and achievements for future employment. A Success Resume functions similarly in the entertainment business.

Unlike other fields, formal schooling and professional certifications count for little here. Because the entertainment industry is larger-than-life and so notoriously superficial, what constitutes a solid achievement is often less straightforward and more difficult to pin down. If we don't keep a record of our accomplishments in music, we may not realize how far we have come or how valuable our credentials truly are. The Success Resume becomes indispensable when we have an opportunity for media or press exposure—or when we are able to connect with investors and larger music entities. It provides a record of who we are and what we have attained.

In years past I received many acknowledgements for my music that I considered insignificant—a write-up in our small local newspaper, a certificate of thanks from a songwriters' group where I had spoken, an email from someone who was touched by one of my songs at a performance. But I soon learned that in the world of showbiz: *No accomplishment is too insignificant to be included in a Success Resume.*

Don't overlook anything—even if, in your own mind, it wasn't that big a deal. Remember: Anything that is not an out-and-out *lie* can be listed as an asset.

> *Often the difference between a minor achievement and a major one consists simply in the way it is reported!*

What Else Can I Do To Build Credibility?

If you are a singer/songwriter and sell your recordings primarily at concert venues and a few local stores, keep a record of your total sales. Get to know your local radio disc jockeys. Send them a promo packet and follow up with phone calls. Volunteer to help with radio sponsored concerts or charity events. DJs appreciate personal contact with artists and, when possible, may include your song in their rotations.

Everywhere you go, wherever there is an opportunity, be ready to place one of your carefully prepared demos and promo packets into the hands of interested people. With each person you meet, comport yourself as a music professional with quality material to offer. Each contact will become another thread in the unique tapestry of influence you are weaving.

If you are a performer as well as a writer, be sure to keep a guest book on the product table at your gigs. Each signature is evidence of that all important fan base so vital for your Success Resume. Start sending out a monthly newsletter updating your fans on your achievements. With email available for free, a newsletter may be drafted and sent with a minimum of time and effort. Keep records of any honors and recognitions you receive for your songwriting and email or fax one page press releases with updates on your latest accomplishments to radio stations and music biz contacts.

No honor or achievement is too unimportant to be included in your Success Resume. It is building your reputation and credibility.

Examples?

The Chicks

A great example of building a Success Resume is Dallas' own gal band, *The Dixie Chicks*. For years, the girls performed at every gig they could find in the DFW area—birthdays, bar mitzvahs—even on street corners. No event was too lowly for the *Chicks*! But with each gig they tightened their sound; they learned what their audiences liked and didn't like; they built their confidence; they honed their shtick to perfection; they kept adding to their mailing list, which grew to a vast database of consumers who purchased their records. They built their success one-gig-at-a-time until finally a major label took note of the incredible buzz they'd generated and began to pursue them. The rest—as they say—is history!

Monkeying to Success

One of the most amazing contemporary success stories is that of a British band called *The Arctic Monkeys*. As recently as 2002, teenagers Alex Turner and Matthew Helders didn't even have instruments. For Christmas Alex asked for a guitar, Matthew for drums. Shortly afterwards, they added Jamie Cook as rhythm guitarist and Andy Nicholson on bass.

As they began to write songs together, they decided to make their demos available for free download over the Internet. It wasn't long before BBC Radio One became aware of the band. Tabloid press coverage quickly followed. The buzz kept growing until they were playing to sell-out crowds of fans who sang their songs word-for-word–songs that had only been released over the Internet!

The music industry was soon in hot pursuit. For a while the Monkeys actually barred label scouts from their shows. They'd come so far without a record company they hardly felt they needed one. In 2005, they finally agreed to sign with Domino Records and soon thereafter "crossed the pond" to the eager acclaim of their American fan base—most of whom had also discovered them on the World Wide Web. At the time they signed their record deal, their senior member was just 18 years old.

At this writing, it remains to be seen whether the band will live up to the incredible buzz they have generated. Whatever the outcome, the point remains that four young students from Boondocks, UK were able to create an international sensation by growing into business over the Internet.

MercyMe

One more success story—this one hits me close to home. My oldest daughter, Martha, was a friend and high school classmate of a kid from Greenville, Texas, named Bart Millard. Bart had a wonderful voice and an engaging personality and was eager to learn all he could about music and about polishing and perfecting his talent. In college Bart met and teamed up with several other talented musicians to form a Christian Contemporary band they named *MercyMe*. Rather than wait around for destiny or the Christian music industry to discover them, they began creating the music that burned in their hearts, stuff their audiences responded to and clamored for.

The band's popularity grew until they were playing over two hundred dates a year. In 1999 alone, *MercyMe* played for more than two hundred thousand people. They were recording and selling their independently produced CDs, touring and doing all the things that successful major artists do—all on their own without a manager, booking agent or marketing team.

"It took an astonishing set of circumstances to actually convince *MercyMe* that it needed to sign a major label deal," Bart says. But the band finally agreed to sign with INO Records and in the spring of 2002, Bart and *MercyMe* walked home with *three* Dove Awards—for *Song of the Year, Songwriter of the Year* and *Pop Recorded Song of the Year*. Bart's crossover hit song, *I Can Only Imagine*, continues to be covered by other artists and played regularly on radio. *MercyMe* polished their talent, worked hard, and created their own success by blooming right where they were planted. CD and ticket sales established this beyond question.

I can't say for sure, but I'll bet you a dollar to a doughnut that INO Records' interest in *MercyMe* was sparked as much by the band's proven success as by their musical talent. And the experience that *MercyMe* gained as independents prepared the band for the professional challenges that lay ahead.

All of this is to assure you, out there in Boondocks, Montana, that success can start for you today—right where you are—with whatever you have! Many one-hit wonders were discovered and became celebrities overnight. Because they lacked knowledge and experience, they vanished just as quickly. The lessons you learn, the goals you achieve and the experiences you have—one day at a time—right there in Boondocks will become the foundation for your achievements tomorrow.

We'll have lots more to say about growing into business in chapter eleven where we will offer some out-of-the-box ideas that are working for people all around the country. So whatever you do, keep reading…

REWIND...

~ Growing into business is often less glamorous, but far more sure and sustainable than many going into business ventures.

~ Every city is a music city. Find your own music community through research and networking.

~ Trade on the credibility you have built in Boondocks and add to it through unswerving persistence.

~ Don't be dazzled by the elusive record deal. Many have ended in disaster.

~ Like any other business, the music industry is not just looking for talent but for success.

~ Start building your Success Resume today.

[1] Hunter S. Thompson quote used by permission of The Estate of Hunter S. Thompson/ The Gonzo Trust. All rights reserved. © 2005, The Estate of Hunter S. Thompson/ The Gonzo Trust.

[2] Wynonna Judd, *Coming Home to Myself*, p. 188 © Wynonna Judd 2005

[3] Joy Bennett Kinnon, *The Rise and Fall of Toni Braxton*, Ebony, December 2000 © Johnson Pub./Gale Group

10

Songplugging From Boondocks

By now you may be seriously reconsidering what it means to be a success in the music industry.

You've wet your feet in the vast sea of music publishing, and have learned that many so-called golden opportunities are more fool's gold than fourteen karat! You know what a recording costs and how to create a high quality CD on a shoestring. You're learning how to develop your unique shtick and to use the credibility you have in your own hometown to leverage your music goals.

But while you are successfully growing into business in Boondocks, there remain a few unanswered questions, like…

How Do I Get My Song To A Major Artist?

Every new song a songwriter writes is the best one yet. It would be perfect for _____ (you can fill in the blank with the name of your favorite artist). But how to get it to her….ah, there's the rub…especially if you're acting as your own publisher and you live in Boondocks.

In this chapter we will take a look at some ways to make contact with a major artist. They are time-tested and can be very effective. You should learn to use them and use them well. I have myself used each of the approaches we'll discuss. They have helped me contact artists, producers and songwriters I never dreamed I would meet in this lifetime.

Of course, they require practice and tenacity—just like anything else in music—and a little serendipity thrown in along the way. You will make mistakes, but they will not be fatal. Just get up, brush yourself off and try again. Let's get started…

Who You Gonna Call?

Some wise person once said that everyone in the world is just three phone calls away. Does that seem crazy? It really isn't. Stay tuned…here's how…

Do the Research

The first step is to find the name of the record company your artist is signed to. Go down to the local bricks-and-mortar record store or do an Internet search. Find the artist's most recent CD and look for the name of the record label that released it.

Next, find the record company's phone number. You may want to consult a music directory for phone numbers and contact information. You may be able to find this information on the record label website. If all else fails, call directory assistance and ask for the company's main number.

Call The Record Label

When the receptionist answers the phone, ask for the promotions department. Promotions is the branch of the record company that links artists with possible concert bookings. Identify yourself confidently. (Remember…you are a trained professional. You can do this!) Ask the promotions department for contact information on your artist's management company. They will usually be happy to give it to you because you may be a big promoter or booking agent who wants to book the artist for a high-paying event.

Call the Manager

Now call the management company and ask to speak to the person who manages your artist. When that person comes to the phone, give your name and identify yourself as a music publisher. Ask where the artist is in her recording schedule. Is she looking for material now? If so, what tempos or styles? If not, when will she be recording again? Tell the manager you have a song you would like to send for the artist's consideration and inquire about her policy for receiving submissions.

Incidentally, if the manager is unavailable and doesn't come to the phone, ask to be put through to her voicemail. Leave your name and phone number with a short message giving the reason for your call. Tell her that you will try to reach her again tomorrow…or next week. Keep calling until you connect.

When you make contact, the manager may tell you to send the song directly to her, in which case be sure to confirm a correct mailing address. Ask the manager how she spells her name and whether there are any special instructions for posted submissions. Some companies require that specific codes be written on the outside of the packages before they are ever opened. Or…the manager may tell you that all submissions go through the A&R Department of the artist's record label.

Call the A&R Rep

Time for another vocabulary word: A&R simply means *Artist and Repertoire*.

The A&R Department is responsible for finding hit material for artists on the label. If the artist's manager tells you that all submissions must go through the A&R Department, politely ask her to give you the name of the A&R representative you should contact. Thank the manager for this information and volunteer to send her a couple of copies of the song anyway—one for the manager and one for that other shadowy figure, the artist's attorney! The more people connected with your artist that hear the song, the better the chance your artist will also hear it.

Now, you have a tremendous advantage! You have the name of the A&R representative who works with your artist. When you call the record company again, you can ask for the A&R person directly. Tell her that Bianca at BigWig Management Company directed you to them. (The more names you can drop, the better.) Repeat your inquiry about submissions and ask for permission to send your song. If they tell you to go ahead and send it, again, be sure to confirm correct procedure, address, name spelling, any identification codes, etc.

What If They Just Say No?

If you are baldly rejected—if you are told that no unsolicited submissions will be accepted—*ever*—don't lose heart.

Start keeping a log of the places you have called and the people with whom you have spoken. Wait three to six months and then call again. Chances are—because of the high employee turnover in music companies—the person you spoke with today will be gone the next time you call.

No matter how impolite the voices on the phone may be, determine that you will never burn bridges by getting irritated or ugly. Be sure to jot down and remember the names of secretaries and administrative assistants. Nothing is so flattering for an administrative assistant as to have a caller remember her by name. I can't tell you how many songs have been cut because a secretary or an intern moved a writer's submission to the top of the pile or gave the song a little plug. Especially in the music business—today's secretary may be tomorrow's record mogul.

Remember: Survival builds credibility like nothing else can. (See chapter nine)

If you continue to present yourself with professionalism and confidence and always pitch excellent material, you will eventually begin to chisel some chips out of the impenetrable wall known as the music industry.

Yikes...What If They Say Yes?

When you receive a green light to send in your song, don't panic. Take some long deep breaths and do what you know to do.

Be sure your package says "professionalism and class." Always include a typewritten lyric sheet and make certain your contact information is featured on both the lyric sheet and the CD demo itself. (Go back to chapter four for a refresher on assembling the presentation.)

Before you put the demo in the mailer, make a point of listening to it one last time just to be sure there are no glitches in the recording. Then take the package to the post office and mail or FedEx the dang thing. I think it's a good idea to use Priority Mail, something with a priority packing appearance. You've put so much work into this already; it's unwise to go cheap on shipping now.

After a couple of weeks, it is appropriate to phone your contact and confirm receipt of the package. Ask for feedback. Be brief and pleasant but persistent. Until they say, "No, we can't use your song," you are still in the running.

What If I'm Just Plain Terrified?

I know that this all may sound very scary to you. If so, you may want to practice a few times before you start making those important phone calls. It's a matter of crossing the inertial threshold and simply doing what you gotta do. Believe me, it gets easier.

Remember: Those people on the other end of the phone are not any smarter or better than you are. They are not larger than life. They are just folks!

The Email Option

I have found email to be a very effective way to contact music executives. There are two good reasons for using it. First, it's a lot less scary for you. Secondly, it's more convenient for the executive who may not have time to take your phone call during a busy business day.

Many receptionists will gladly provide a company email address for the person you are trying to reach. Some will not. It doesn't hurt to ask…all they can say is "No."

Music directories are also a good source for the names and email addresses of people holding key positions in the music business. (You'd be amazed at how many emails I receive by way of response from someone doing Internet correspondence at 3:00 AM.) A well-written email inquiring about upcoming recording projects and artists may get a response when all else fails. (More about music directories later in this chapter.)

One rule that I adhere to religiously is this:

> *Never send any submission (by mail or by MP3) unless you have first made personal contact and obtained permission to send it.*

This is extremely important because most music professionals are inundated with unsolicited material every day. If you don't make a personal connection first, your submission will not be expected or welcome. Unsolicited MP3 files are especially irritating because they take up lots of room in the receiver's email program. Because they are unsolicited it is unknown whether they may contain viruses. Most music pros won't even open such attachments.

For the songwriter, unsolicited submissions mean wasted time and effort. They also scream "amateur" and undermine the credibility you have been working so hard to build.

Don't send anything unsolicited!

How Do Real Publishers Pitch Songs?

What are you talking about? You *are* a real publisher! If you don't believe that, go back to the beginning of this book and review.

When a music publisher in a major music city signs a song, she usually produces a demo and then begins to pitch the song to her contacts in the music industry. Sometimes she does this herself. Sometimes she uses songpluggers.

Songpluggers

Many major publishers have staff people called songpluggers whose job it is to copy demos and lyric sheets, create promo packages and make sure a publisher's songs are heard by those in charge of evaluating material for upcoming recordings.

Pluggers in big music cities may schedule sit-down appointments to discuss songs with the artists, producers and managers concerned. These are, of course, ideal because they allow the plugger to interact personally with those making the decisions. If a personal appointment is not possible, the plugger often sends a demo package by mail—usually with identifying code numbers or words that let the recipient know the package is from a recognized source.

What the music publisher and the plugger do is what you are already doing if you have been applying the suggestions in this book. You are making good, clear demos of your songs; you are presenting them in promo packages that indicate good taste and professional sophistication; and you are networking with members of your local music community to locate artists and producers looking for material.

Independent Songplugging Services

Of course, there is a clear advantage to being in the right place at the right time. You may be plugging like crazy to artists in Boondocks, but what about recording opportunities in other places—especially in distant music cities?

There are independent songplugging services that specialize in representing independent writers and publishers. They are usually retained for a monthly fee that varies depending on the number of songs they represent from your catalog. As with anything else in the music business: let the buyer beware. While there are many reputable and trustworthy pluggers, there are many who are all too quick to collect a retainer but slow to work your catalog. If you are thinking about using an independent songplugging service:

Ask for a list of their clients—and then, don't be afraid to call those clients for references. Ask questions like:

♪ *How long have you used this service?*

♪ *Are you satisfied with the job they are doing for you?*

♪ *Have you had any cuts by major artists?*

♪ *Have you had any cuts by independent artists?*

♪ *Have you made at least enough money in royalties to pay for the pluggers' fees?*

Like music publishers, some songpluggers are well established with many high level contacts that offer great opportunities for song placement. They are, of course, more expensive to retain. Smaller pluggers may not have the same access, but they may make up for it with their commitment to your catalog and hard work.

Request a tracking list that shows when and where your songs were pitched—and the response obtained.

Expect enthusiasm about your songs. Your plug-gers should be as familiar with your catalog as you are. They should believe in your songs and pitch them aggressively.

Have a clear contract with your pluggers for a well-defined period of time (term). Consider an initial six-month to twelve-month term. This allows your pluggers to get to know your catalog and gain momentum pitching it. Often these contracts can be worded to renew automatically if both parties are happy with the arrangement.

Beside the retainer, you can expect to pay your pluggers in the event they are successful in placing your song(s). Some will request a percentage of any royalties generated. Others require specific cash bonuses if a song reaches certain benchmark numbers in sales (gold, platinum etc.). Be sure you under-stand the contract and are completely comfortable with it. It would be wise to have it reviewed by an experienced entertainment attorney.

Any Other Tips To Help Me As I Plug Along?

Effective songplugging involves staying informed about who is recording and what kinds of songs they are looking for. Mainstream publishers in major music cities have the advantage of a local, professional communication net-work that gives them the inside edge when it comes to placing songs. There are, however, a couple of tools available to you—the independent—as you plug away from Boondocks.

Tip Sheets

Professional tip sheets are publications that let you know about upcoming recordings and the kinds of songs being considered for them. There are tip sheets for every genre of music, and while subscriptions can be a little pricey, they are one of the best ways to stay abreast of recording projects and artists seeking new material.

Music Directories

Professional music business directories list the names, titles, addresses, phone numbers and email accounts of key executives at major record labels and independents alike. They can be expensive, but they are essential if you intend to make contact with people inside the industry who can get your songs to major recording artists.

Look through directories carefully and note the different departments in each company. Most appoint directors to each of the music styles the company produces. For example, if you are an R&B songwriter, note the name of the A&R Director for R&B. Then make contact with that person by phone or email and inquire about which of their artists will be recording in the near future. Ask for permission to send a few of your songs for consideration.

One other tip...

> *As you begin to make contact with record labels, be aware that all record companies represent both well-known artists and newer, not-so-well-known artists. The latter may be much more accessible and willing to consider outside material than more established artists who already have favorite writers. By getting to know artists before they become household names, you may be able to grow with them, providing that great song that pushes them into national prominence.*

Music Periodicals

Well-known international music periodicals like *Billboard Magazine, Rolling Stone, Performing Songwriter* and *American Songwriter* are terrific sources of news on trends in the music industry. They give you an education in the culture of music. You may find some subscriptions costly, but as we mentioned in chapter two, the more involved you are, the more expensive this whole business is likely to become. You *will* find a way to fund this deal if you really want to.

Some periodicals offer online subscriptions at a fraction of the cost. Visit their websites and look at the special offers. Think of it this way…it beats a ticket to LA, NYC or Nashville, and it may be far more informative.

For our recommendations on tip sheets, music registries and music periodicals, visit our website at **www.FromNowhereWithNothing.com**.

Stay in Touch

Get familiar with names that keep turning up in music directories and on tip sheets and keep track of people you meet by phone and email. Make a note of career changes and promotions among your contacts and stay in touch. Never lose contact.

Several years ago I met by telephone an A&R representative at one of the major labels. He was an underling—just another employee in a large A&R department. One day I called and discovered he was no longer with the company. Rather than losing touch with him, I inquired after his whereabouts and was told he had moved to another major record label. When I called the new label to tell him I had heard of his move and that I wanted to stay in touch, I discovered he was no longer an underling. In fact, he'd been appointed vice president. Now I had an influential contact—and a friend as well. That's the way it works.

How About Making Trips To Major Music Cities?

Another way out-of-town songwriters promote their material is by making regular visits to major music cities to network with publishers, producers and A&R representatives.

When I first got serious about songwriting more than twenty years ago, trips to music cities were considered indispensable. As years passed and music companies merged and downsized, it became more and more difficult to make appointments with music professionals—especially if you were an unknown writer from out of town. It can also get darn expensive—especially when you are making trips frequently and they are not accomplishing anything. Before you blow your wad on a plane ticket and hotel expenses, consider the following:

Be Sure You are Ready

The prospect of traveling to LA, New York or Nashville can be an exciting one for any aspiring songwriter. Stories of writers walking into major recording or publishing companies and walking out with deals are the stuff of urban legend. They are more fantasy than truth.

Many aspiring songwriters make such trips prematurely—before their songs are up to competitive standard. Remember that music executives in publishing companies and record labels are used to hearing hit-quality songs by successful songwriters every day. If you are fortunate enough to book an appointment with an executive at a major company, be sure your songs are well-crafted and buffed to a high sheen. They will need to hold their own against pros with appointments later that day.

*Remember: You never have a second chance to
make a first impression!*

Get Feedback First

The excitement of writing them makes it difficult to be objective about your songs. You may think your latest creation is the hit of the century—and it may well be. But be sure to get knowledgeable feedback first!

We discussed the importance of feedback at length in chapter three. It is critical you get it now—*before you make your trip*. There will only be time to play a few of your songs during appointments with publishers and producers. Be sure that you are leading with your absolute best.

Here is where the professional song critique can be a great help. Someone experienced in songwriting and hip to the current trends in music marketing may be able to help you decide which of your songs are strongest and most commercially viable.

There are many music professionals who offer critiquing services at reasonable fees. That said, you do well to proceed with caution. It is up to you to check the credentials of anyone offering to review your song for a fee. Under no condition should the reviewer promise some kind of publishing or record deal as part of the critiquing fee. This is a shark warning: the waters are infested. Find a different place to swim!

Information on recommended critiquing services can be found on our website at **www.FromNowhereWithNothing.com**.

Plan Your Trip Ahead of Time

When you feel confident that you are ready to make a music trip, think carefully about your timing. Be sure you don't schedule your trip when a big music event is taking place. Don't, for instance, plan to travel during Grammy week. Music execs will not be available for appointments. Do the research and be sure that the week you are in town is a routine one.

Next, try to set up as many appointments as possible from home. If you have met people by phone or email while plugging your songs, start with them. Call and ask if they might be available for a short appointment to listen to a few of your new songs. Perhaps you have only met the secretary or receptionist. That's OK! These people are extremely valuable contacts when it comes to placing songs.

The performing rights organizations (PROs)—ASCAP, BMI or SESAC—have offices in every major music city. If you are not a member of one of these organizations yet, your trip to LA, New York or Nashville can be a great opportunity to shop each of these and determine which best fits your needs.

Call ahead and ask for their *Member Services Department*. Tell them that you are a songwriter trying to make a decision about which PRO to affiliate with. Let them know the dates you will be in town and make an appointment to see one of their representatives. Performing rights organizations were created to assist songwriters. Their representatives may have suggestions and contacts for you to pursue as you seek to place your songs.

Keep Appointments Professionally and Confidently

Driving to your first appointment with a music exec can be one of the most exciting (if not terrifying) moments of your life. Think of this appointment as you would an appointment with a professional in any other business—a banker, a lawyer, a professor.

Approach it with a balance of personal humility and dignified self-confidence. You may be just commencing your career in music and may have a lot to learn, but you have been working hard to perfect your songwriting skills and you should not feel as if you have to kiss up to anyone!

> *Remember: It's the job of the music industry to discover the next great blockbuster hit and performance sensation. You may be that person. It is their loss if they fail to treat you with the respect you deserve.*

Dress appropriately. Arrive on time. If the music publisher or producer has agreed to hear some of your songs, be sure your professionally produced demos are ready to present and easily accessible so you don't have to fumble around to find them. With any luck your songs will spark real interest but if the publisher isn't wowed by your work, don't lose heart. These people hear songs all day, every day, and may simply decide to pass on your song without comment. If this should happen, don't be afraid to ask what precisely they're looking for and what you might do to improve your songs. If suggestions are made, express your willingness to go home and re-write. Ask if you may re-submit your songs with changes.

Have Realistic Expectations

As you plan and make your music journey, expect an educational experience…expect to meet new people…expect a certain amount of rejection and disappointment but don't expect to be discovered and made a star overnight. It will likely take dozens of trips before you network your way to the right people and access major label artists. Enjoy the journey and the adventures you have along the way. Keep a journal of the people you meet and the experiences you have. Who knows? Maybe one day you will write a book called *How To Get Somewhere in the Music Business from Nowhere with Nothing (the Sequel)*.

SUMMING UP

In this chapter we have examined a few of the traditional procedures for pitching songs and having them signed. It's been done like this for years, and will continue to be done this way for at least the foreseeable future. You should become familiar—and proficient—with the various strategies.

As we have said, the music industry is in a state of unprecedented transition. The Internet and other technologies have created amazing opportunities for songwriters and artists to get their music to the world. If we hope to be part of the music industry in the new millennium, it is essential that we pursue both traditional and out-of-the-box approaches—*anything* to advance our songs. The more dominoes, the better the likelihood that one will tip and begin the cascade to success.

In the next chapter we will examine some fresh and creative ways songwriters are making music, making money and making history!

REWIND...

~ While you are busily growing into business in Boondocks, you can pursue connections with major artists and music companies using traditional strategies with a proven track record.

~ No matter how important an artist or music professional may be, they are really only a few phone calls or emails away. Learn how to find correct contact information and use it well.

~ Independent songplugging services are a good option for pitching your catalog in distant cities.

~ Utilize music directories, tip sheets and periodicals to keep yourself abreast of what is happening in the business and where your songs might have a shot.

~ Consider making a trip to one of the major music cities only after you have carefully prepared and planned for it.

11

Creative Connections

When all is said and done, successful songs are really about one very simple but profound thing—*connection*.

A successful song is one that has found a way to effectively communicate the ideas and emotions of the songwriter to the hearts of listeners, whether a stadium full of them or just one heartbroken motorist on a backcountry road. If a song touches an emotional chord it is a success!

> *The basic task of every songwriter is to get the songs out of her heart and into the hearts of other people—hopefully lots of other people (cause there's nothing wrong with making a living at this, right?)*

We've been learning a lot about creating and promoting songs through the intelligent use of recording and computer technology. What remains a challenge for the independent is distribution and marketing—finding a way to let listeners know about your music and making it easy for them to acquire it.

So How Do I Get My Music Out There?

The answer to this question is limited only by your imagination.

Because major labels have national and international distribution networks that can move a lot of product and generate large sales, they are widely perceived as the ticket to success for artists. But it's important to remember that major label projects involve a large overhead expense because of the many employees who must be paid from the sales of recordings. Independent artists, on the other hand, have little or no overhead—no middlemen waiting for their salary checks. When an independent achieves even modest distribution, she recoups production costs and begins to generate an amazing profit in very little time. The key is coming up with creative ways to move your recordings!

It is here that many otherwise very talented songwriters and musicians simply lose heart. They have convinced themselves that marketing and distribution are impossible without a major recording contract or publishing deal. Whenever I encounter this line of thinking, I call, "Bull$@#* !"

> *If you are creative enough to have written a great song, you are creative enough to come up with a way to get it to the ears of listeners! You simply turn your creativity loose in another direction and think outside-the-box.*

But What If I Don't Know Anything About Business?

If you don't know the basics of business—learn.

There are classes and seminars offered all the time both live and online that teach you how to run a business of any kind—even a music business. They are affordable and accessible. You are an intelligent and competent individual.

There is no excuse for failing to acquire the skills you need to promote and market your music and yourself.

Determination and Destiny

Several years ago I had the privilege of an extended visit with Mathew Knowles, father of Beyonce and genius behind the multi-platinum girls' trio, *Destiny's Child*. (You met him back in chapter nine at the NARAS meeting.)

Mathew recalled that in the 1980s when Beyonce was very young, he and his wife, Tina, were told by Beyonce's dance teacher that their child had an incredible gift. As Beyonce won more and more dance competitions in their hometown of Houston and throughout Texas, Mathew and Tina knew they had a responsibility to help this special child achieve her full potential.

The only problem was…they knew nothing about the entertainment industry or the music business. Mathew sold equipment for Xerox. Tina was the owner of an upscale hair salon. Where in the world would they begin learning all they needed to know to guide their gifted daughter?

What about Houston Community College?

Mathew Knowles went down to the local community college and signed up for a course called *Survey of the Music Business*—taught by Dr. Aubrey Tucker. Dr. Tucker recalls that Mathew was "like a sponge," soaking up everything he could learn about the music industry and putting it together with what he already knew from his experience in sales.

Growing into business from where they were with what they had, Mathew and Tina turned their home into a training camp where Beyonce and several of her friends were schooled in the various disciplines required for success in music—vocals, choreography, and stage technique. They learned interviewing skills. Tina sewed costumes and did the girls' hair. Together the parents toted the girls to competitions, concerts, performances and interviews. They learned as they grew. Mathew now runs a music empire that includes a management firm, record label and production studio—all right there in Houston, not too far from Houston Community College where he took his first course. Enough said about that!

But What If I'm Just Too Right-Brained For Business?

If you find that you simply don't have the business chops to make money with your music, link up with someone who does.

Case In Point

Several years ago I read about a songwriter who wrote beautiful, relaxing, instrumental, New Age music. He was a gifted composer and producer and was able to create his own CDs in his home studio, but he was a total klutz when it came to figuring out where to go from there.

So, he contacted an old college buddy who had a master's degree in marketing but knew absolutely nothing about the music industry (that, as it turned out was probably his strongest asset). The way his buddy figured it, this was just another product to promote and sell. He looked around at the market and came up with an idea.

Every year major corporations give Christmas packages to their employees. These packages contain annual bonus checks together with some other Christmas goodies or gifts. The marketing guy approached one of the largest companies in the area and sold them on the idea of including his friend's CDs as part of the Christmas package. There were 4000 employees in the company—4000 CDs in one sale! The CDs were such a hit with the employees that the company did it again the following year and the one after that! The musician made enough in the first sale to record two follow-up albums. That's thinking outside the CD case.

But Was That Just Luck?

Nope! I've got dozens of stories like this. Each one of them proves that *the harder you work, the more you innovate...the luckier you get.*

Love Songs and Lingerie

A local singer-songwriter in a major US city writes and records romantic ballads. Several years ago he came up with the idea of asking a local retail store to carry his recordings in their lingerie department. As shoppers checked out of the store with their lingerie purchases, the countertop display of romantic music CDs caught their eye. This marketing strategy proved a big hit. The singer-songwriter had found a great way to cash in on the mood shoppers were in when they bought their sexy lingerie.

He sold so many CDs he became a phenomenon in his community and has had incredible opportunities to perform his music across the state. The amazing profits provided a very nice living and allowed him to continue doing his music his way. He was able to touch the hearts of many listeners without ever leaving his home state. Would you consider him successful? I sure would!

Vicki Logan and Her Moo-ed Music

While writing this chapter, I received a phone call from Vicki Logan, an artist inquiring about song critiquing services. As we visited I was quickly mesmerized by the story of how she began writing and recording songs.

Vicki described herself as a middle-aged, slightly overweight housewife from Minnesota who had always had dreams of becoming a songwriter. After going through a divorce and facing the demands of single parenthood, Vicki remarried and was given a keyboard by her husband.

Here, in her own words, is an account of her amazing journey:

> *I wasn't raised in poverty; I wasn't the victim of a horrible crime. As a matter of fact, I'm an average person out there leading a relatively normal life. So what's so special about me? You'll see…*
>
> *"You're an overweight, middle-aged mom. You won't be going anywhere." I seemed to hear that phrase over and over at the beginning of my musical journey. Most people in the music industry felt that if I didn't have the image, according to the major music industry players, then I didn't have any talent. I thought the music industry was about music?*

I had dabbled with the piano for several years but never took lessons or pursued anything, so I made up my own songs by ear because I couldn't read regular sheet music. People really seemed to like them so I thought to myself, "Why don't you do something with this?"

Like most of us, self-doubt set in because I reacted to the media and the industry. I didn't fit the part. My husband said, "So what! It's not about the media's image. It's about the people you touch with your music." And he was absolutely right. I decided to follow my dream and release a CD of original music. Really, what was stopping me?

I did the research and found out where to record, who to work with, how to get the material pressed into a product, did the graphic design work, took some photos. Hey…before I knew what happened, I had done it. I had "Chasing Dreams", my first full-length album.

I sent it out to a few radio stations and to some contests. It was aired and I won a few. It was a nice little ego boost. Then I got my first record contract. I learned a ton from that contract during the next two years. I realized that the music industry was changing drastically and that I needed to change with it to grow as an artist and business person. Being signed to the label didn't allow me that luxury so I terminated my contract with them.

My next CD, "Finding My Way", was released in 2003 on my very own label and ended up on New Age Reporter's Top 100 Albums of 2003 Chart. I had over 800 radio stations airing the music by now as well as licensing to several syndicated programs. The Internet garnered me two Number One songs on AOL Radio for over 21 weeks and 6 weeks respectively. My third CD, "The Ride", did the same for 2004 and actually climbed a bit higher on the chart. It also increased radio airplay to over 1000 stations worldwide.

To my amazement, I dropped into yet another niche while pursuing my dream—Moo-ed Music as we've begun to label it from a Pioneer Press article released in Minneapolis/ St. Paul. Apparently, at one of the events I attended some farmers liked the music and began to play it in their barns. The cows enjoyed it so much that they produced more milk! People ask if I'm offended. Heck no! If the farmers didn't like it, well, the cows would never have had the chance to hear it.

I could go on here, but the point to the story is that we must be true to ourselves. We must follow our dreams and do the things we know we are capable of doing. When we don't do them, we allow misperceptions and stereotypes to rule our lives. We feed into the system that keeps us down. It doesn't matter that we cannot please everyone in the world, but it does matter if we can help even just one.

I do what I do because I love it. My reward is knowing that I have inspired even just one person to do what it is they love, or have helped even one overcome a bump in life's journey. I have made a positive dif-ference...and it wasn't because of my weight, my looks, what I have or don't. It was all because I am me. If we could all just take that first step, believe in ourselves, be ourselves and help that one person, I wonder just how much we might change the world.

If that story doesn't inspire you, I'd suggest that you check your pilot light—it may have gone out!

For more information visit Vicki's website at **www.VickiLogan.com**.

Using What's Between Your Ears

There are opportunities for success all over the place—just like there are great song ideas everywhere, floating in the air.

> *Creativity has less to do with inventing some-thing new, than with programming your mind to see the potential all around you.*

Here's one of my favorite Success-Is-Right-Under-Your-Nose Stories:

Kay Seamayer, affectionately known to her friends and fans as KC, is a sixty-something singer-songwriter-grandmother and a fellow member of the Dallas Songwriters Association. After the September 11th tragedy, she expressed the mix of emotions she was feeling in a song called *Let Freedom Ring*. She produced a professional demo and took all the right steps to get her song heard by music publishers and professionals, but it was roundly rejected. So KC began to look for another way up the mountain.

She went to her computer and typed the words "let freedom ring" into a search engine. The search yielded a host of references—the Martin Luther King speech with that line as its distinctive refrain, a book with that title and others. Among them, one that piqued KC's interest: the Annual Let Freedom Ring National Bell Ringing Ceremony of the Liberty Bell, sponsored by the Pennsylvania Society of Sons of the Revolution in Philadelphia. Bingo!

KC placed an MP3 file of her song on her website. She sent the link and a cover letter introducing her song "to whom it may concern" at the Philadelphia Society of the Sons of the Revolution. The email and song link landed in the hands of Shirley Sadak, the executive director.

Result? KC was invited to perform her song at the Annual July Fourth National Bell Ringing Ceremony in Philadelphia, where she has performed it every year since. She has sung her song before Supreme Court judges and dignitaries. She has sung her song with the Philadelphia Boys Choir providing background vocals. She has sung with concert bands and choirs at the National Cemetery, the World War II D-Day Museum in New Orleans, the National Day of Prayer, and the Veteran's Administration V-J Day Celebration. She sang recently in New York at a World Trade Center Survivors Network Commemorative Service remembering those who lived and died in the Oklahoma City and World Trade Center bombings.

KC promoted her song so successfully that she has since started her own sheet music publishing company where she makes all arrangements available as PDF electronic files over the Internet.

All because she typed her song title into a search engine. Now don't you wish you had thought of that?

For more information on KC's creative ideas and adventures visit her online at **www.LetFreedomRingPublishing.com**.

I could keep telling you stories out the yin-yang about enterprising and resourceful artists I have met who are making a living doing the music they love. I am absolutely confident the same is possible for anyone willing to work hard and unleash creative energies when it comes to promotion. It ain't easy...but it's great fun!

Taking It to the Streets

The promotional ideas we have discussed thus far might all be addressed in a course called *Hurdle Jumping Techniques.* Between writing your song and seeing it become a blockbuster hit that connects with millions of people, there extends a long and winding path peppered with hurdles. One by one, we have been finding ways around them or over them.

Until the mid-nineties, the hurdle marked *distribution* was almost insurmountable for independent artists. Only major labels could ensure that recordings found a way to the average consumer. But that's not the case today. The old paradigm is shattering. The playing field is being leveled. Artists are taking their music to the streets and connecting with fans—*and they're doing it without major labels.*

Keep in mind that if you are an independent artist—creating your own CDs—you only have to recoup your raw production and manufacturing costs before you begin to turn a profit. If you are a gigging artist/writer, you have a wonderful opportunity to distribute your recordings at your own performances. Offer a special for people in the audience...something like: *buy three CDs and get one free.* Once you have recouped your expenses, you can begin generating up to 85-90 percent profit per unit of sale—a far greater percentage than artists signed to major labels.

I know you may be thinking that all of this sounds pretty good on paper. In point of fact, the bookings may be a little thin these days. Where are you going to do all these performances and sell your CDs?

How about a *house concert?*

What The Heck Is A House Concert?

It's just one of the most combustible new phenomena in the music world today—that's all. Now, don't feel like a klutz if you've never heard of a house concert. Neither had I until a couple of years ago.

Musical House Calls

One day as I was busy at my daily ritual of deleting spam, I noticed an email from someone named David Byboth who was hosting house concerts regularly in his suburban Dallas home. The concert he was promoting at the time featured an artist/writer named Richard Leigh. If you don't recognize his name, you will probably remember his million-selling hit Country song *Don't It Make My Brown Eyes Blue?*, which won the Grammy for Best Country Song in 1978 and was named one of the Ten Most Performed Songs of the Century by ASCAP in 1999.

My son, David, and I decided to see what all this house concert hype was about, and we attended. We discovered something wonderful—very old, yet very new—people gathering in a home to enjoy music together. When we left the concert several hours later we agreed that it was one of the most engaging and rewarding musical events either of us had ever experienced. Here's the way it worked:

The host opened his home to a living room full of people—somewhere between 20 to 40 people on folding chairs. The tickets were $20 a piece. Each concertgoer brought something to eat—sorta like a mini-potluck (chips and salsa, a dessert or a bottle of wine). The goodies were placed in the kitchen for later.

Then the artist, Richard Leigh, appeared. He required very little in the way of props or equipment—just a simple sound system and a stool. He had his own guitar. For the next hour and a half he sang his songs, told the stories behind them and completely captivated us all. Instead of having to view him through binoculars from the nosebleed section of a concert hall, we all just sort of hung out together in a relaxed and intimate setting.

At the end of the first set, we took a break. We broke open the goodies in the kitchen and chatted with each other while Richard sold and autographed his CDs. Then back to the living room for another hour of incredible entertainment. By the end of the evening, we felt we had been in a gathering of friends. We had connected with the music and with each other.

Is This Some Kind Of New Fad?

Actually, it has been around for centuries.

Remember, I said several chapters back that music is not just a product…it's part of our cells and our souls. It will always find a way to be shared. Think about times past—before the days of electronic over-stimulation. People would gather around the piano or harpsichord in the parlor after dinner to listen as someone played the tunes of the day. Or they would sing together, harmonizing as they were able. Through wars and famines…in joy and in sorrow… people have found a way to connect with each other through music no matter what obstacles stand in the way.

Irresistible Force Meets Immovable Object

When it comes to obstacles, here's a whopper for you. Consider the immovable object of bigotry that divided America during the days of segregation. Whatever difficulties you have faced so far in your musical journey, chances are they pale in comparison to the hardships gifted African-American musicians faced during the decades leading up to the Civil Rights Movement.

Recently, I had lunch with my friend, Vaneese Thomas, a well-known and sought-after vocalist and songwriter. Vaneese has recorded with music legends in every genre including Sting, Eric Clapton, Luther Vandross, Jonathan Butler, Phil Collins, Michael McDonald and many others. She is the daughter of famed R&B legend, Rufus Thomas—who was part of the emerging Memphis music scene during the forties and fifties when segregation was in full effect.

As our conversation turned to the "new" phenomenon of house concerts, Vaneese remarked that the concept is one that was used extensively by

African-American artists prior to integration. Barred from large venues catering to white audiences, black artists created their own network for distributing and promoting music. An artist would come to town and usually stay with a local resident. Word would go out through the grassroots—one person telling another. People would meet wherever there was a place to hold them—venues that became known as juke joints. Some of the greatest artists of the twentieth century emerged during those difficult days.

Refusing to be impeded by a dysfunctional society, African-American artists wrote and played music that became an irresistible force. That force overcame the immovable object. They flouted prejudice to express themselves artistically and connect with the hearts of listeners. They created their own successes—writing and playing songs under the radar, or so it seemed. By the time the laws enforcing legal segregation were abolished, theirs was already the popular music of the day. It had played an indispensable part in bringing the old racist order to its knees.

Where there is a will…and a song…there is *always, always, always* a way.

For more information on Vaneese Thomas and her soul-stirring music, visit **www.PeacefulWaters.com**.

The Texas Connection

The house concert was always one of your less conspicuous music events or happenings—until recently. But it was always a part of the scene. Here in my own home state of Texas house concerts have become a big part of our music tradition over the last quarter century, springing out of the annual Kerrville Folk Festival and the Folk Alliance.

One of the most famous hosts was Bruce Rouse, a passionate Folk music fan, who opened his Austin home to hundreds of artists and thousands of folk music fans over the years. Bruce helped others to grasp the vision for house concert promotion and mentored many of the new artists who passed through his doors. His unexpected death in 2005 was a huge loss to the community, but the seeds Bruce planted have continued bearing fruit—not only in Texas, and not just in Folk music—but across the country and in every genre.

Sometimes it takes a while to get a smoldering fire to blaze. It takes time and stirring up and a little more fuel, but once it catches on, watch out!

But Why Would a Famous Artist Do House Concerts?

For the same reasons that aspiring artists do them—because they are musically rewarding and financially profitable. That's why.

A little Internet research will reveal how the house concert network is spreading like wildfire. Let's just take a few minutes to examine the benefits for everyone involved.

The Hosts

♫ Frequently, hosts are interested in some aspect of music and hope to develop their own talents by interacting with the artists they host. Many hosts record their house concerts and learn something about sound engineering in the process. They may eventually become producers with their own home studios.

♫ Hosts often donate a portion of ticket sales to a local charity, allowing them to support their communities and indulge their love of music in one go.

♫ As the house concert movement expands, hosts receive well-deserved recognition. In some circles awards are presented for the Best Venue. (The experience of hosting is so positive some have purchased homes with more square footage to accommodate concertgoers and host performing artists with greater ease.)

The Attendees

♫ House concert attendees have a delightful musical experience like the one my son and I enjoyed with Richard Leigh at David Byboth's home.

They gather in a relaxed and intimate setting where a connection is made with the music, the artist and other listeners.

♫ House concertgoers experience the magic of discovery. Since the advent of file sharing and music downloads, fans have been approaching their music differently. A decade ago it was the high visibility promotions of major labels that drove sales. Today, fans are keen to find exciting new talent and new venues for themselves, following a buzz online or the word-of-mouth recommendations of friends. House concerts allow audiences to discover artists and get to know them as individuals—up close and personal—often before they become household names.

♫ House concert venues in residential settings are an attractive alternative to urban clubs and arenas where parking may be costly or difficult to find and crime is more prevalent.

The Artists

♫ Featured house concert artists get to do their own music their own way, sharing original songs as well as the stories behind them. This is an extremely powerful motivator—even for nationally-known artists—and an enjoyable way to fill in dead days between major cities in the midst of a larger concert tour.

♫ Financial profits are substantial for artists. They receive ticket sales (minus any charitable donations) plus CD sales. (You can do the math…$20 tickets…40 people or more…plus CD sales…can mean close to a grand an evening).

♫ The artist enjoys comfortable bed and breakfast in the host's home.

♫ Word-of-mouth drives the house concert grassroots movement. A dedicated fan base evolves that is invested in the artist whom they love as a musician, and whom they have come to know as a person. Marketing moguls have long agreed that word-of-mouth is the absolute best promotional strategy in the world. It's powerful!

♫ The artist becomes part of the house concert underground. Whatever the genre or style of music, there are hosts across the country and even overseas who are looking to book their next event. Connections multiply with each new concert—for artists, for hosts and for listeners.

Spend a couple of hours Googling "house concerts." Here are some websites to get you started: **www.HouseConcerts.org**; **www.HouseConcerts.com** and **www.ConcertsInYourHome.com**.

You'll find all kinds of incredible information that will stimulate your creativity and spark ideas for your own music. Variations on this theme are limitless and can work for any style or genre.

If you have a house—or you know someone who does—you have no excuse. *Start planning a house concert now!*

What Are Some Other Ways To Distribute And Market Music?

Don't Overlook the Obvious

Don't forget about your local retailers—what we call bricks-and-mortar stores.

While many of these chains have closed or merged in the aftermath of the Internet explosion, many retailers continue to carry music products. It's often not as hard to get into these stores as you may think.

Inquire about the local artist policy at book and record stores in your area. Most major chains and independent stores have a section featuring local talent. They will often take your product on consignment for a fixed period of time, or buy it outright for around fifty percent of retail. Offer to do an in-store appearance, performance or CD signing. Remember, merchants are looking for new ways to sell product too. You will find many retailers delighted to set up a date and time for you to be a featured guest. They may announce your performance in their mail-outs and email promotions and may even put up posters in the store. It's all exposure, baby, and that generates buzz, which creates sales.

The Incredible Internet

Whether or not you can get into bricks-and-mortar stores, there is always the Internet. I cannot over emphasize the amazing revolution going on in this medium. The Internet has changed *everything* for independents.

First, there are the major online distributors. Amazon.com was one of the first to begin distributing CDs by independent artists. Today there is a plethora of online retailers who specialize in promoting and distributing serious artists in every genre. The cool thing about these companies is that they process credit cards, fill orders and provide their clients with promotional options—all for a much smaller percentage of the sale than a major distributor would demand. And they make you instantly available to the entire world!

The Internet has opened new and unprecedented opportunities for self-promotion and distribution. Among the most significant of these is the artist's website. Never before in the history of the music business has it been possible for so many aspiring singers/songwriters/bands to offer their music to so many people at such a minimal cost. Your website is dedicated to *you!* You are the star of that piece of virtual real estate and you can present yourself to the world as professionally and creatively as any major label would a household-name artist. A well-designed website creates immediate national and international distribution opportunities and ups your credibility about 1,000 percent.

Avant-garde music publications and websites now direct readers to a musician's or a band's MySpace page where they can find pictures, lyrics, tour dates, discographies and in many cases download free music. *Playlist*, a column in the Sunday edition of the *New York Times* that reports on hip new music (much of it by unsigned talent boasting little more than a buzz on the street) routinely posts hyperlinks to the music blogs of artists it reviews. The links are usually featured in the body of the review itself and can be accessed with the ease of a mouse click in the newspaper's online edition.

The reason for the incredible popularity of services like MySpace, especially among musicians, is that blog pages are easy to create, and they cost you *nada*! Simple step-by-step instructions guide users through the process of creating and launching a site. Your own songs, graphics and text can be easily uploaded and edited into an audiovisual presentation, usually in a matter of minutes. What you get is a web page, dedicated to you as an artist and to getting the word out.

But What If I Don't Know Squat About Internet Technology?

No excuse!

The Internet is probably your best resource for taking your music to the world. In this day and age, you can't afford not to be Internet savvy. You must at least attempt to keep up with the technology of the twenty-first century or you will soon be as extinct as a musical Tyrannosaurus Rex! If it all sounds a little overwhelming, however, let me tell you a story…

Several years ago my husband, Dave, decided he wanted to build a house—that's right, a real house—a house that we would actually live in when it was finished. Now you have to understand that he's not a contractor or builder. He's an author and a teacher, but he has always loved working with his hands and building things. When we moved to Dallas he decided it was time for him to fulfill that lifelong dream. I tried to be supportive (cause I really do believe the man can do anything) but when I watched the foundation being poured, I have to say I was a little doubtful. How would Dave handle things like framing, sheet rocking, plumbing, electrical installation and the myriad of other jobs required to build a house?

He was soon so far embarked on his house-building project that there could be no turning back. One night, I asked him tentatively, "How can you be so sure you have the skills you need to do all this?" His answer was one of those freeze-frame moments you know you will never forget. "Hey, look at the guys who do this stuff," Dave said. "Framers, sheet rockers, plumbers—they're great guys, but they're not rocket scientists. If they can learn how to do these things, so can I!"

Wow! Instead of being overwhelmed by the challenge, Dave had enough confidence in his own intelligence to believe he could learn whatever he needed to learn to get the job done.

And I'll be the first to admit he had the chops for the task at hand. We have lived in the house he built for over twelve years now, and nothing has caved in or fallen apart. The roof hasn't leaked once!

I made a mental note to self that I would try to see new challenges from Dave's perspective instead of from my usual pessimistic viewpoint. It has literally changed my life. Just like anyone else, I approach the learning curve involved in acquiring a new skill with reluctance. It's so much easier to just do the things I know how to do rather than to learn something new. But whenever we venture outside our comfort zone we stretch ourselves. We find brain cells we didn't even know we had. We stimulate mental acuity and creativity.

So back to the artist's website. Don't tell me you can't do it! Start by getting online and browsing through other artists' websites. Note which graphics, colors and styles you think are cool and might be adapted to your site. When you have some ideas try your hand at creating a blog site. They're a snap to design and launch—and it just doesn't get any cheaper than free.

When and if the time comes to create a web site with a broader range of design and merchandising options just flip your internal switch to the setting marked "learning mode." There are software packages that have simplified the process of website development to such an extent that almost anyone who really wants to can learn how to do it. You can sign up for a course at a local community college or read some books on the subject. Like Dave says: "The guys who do this are not rocket scientists!" You are every bit as intelligent as you need to be to grasp this stuff.

It all comes down to whether or not you have that fire in your belly to communicate your songs to others. If so, you will do whatever you have to do to make it happen—including building a website. If you get stuck, find someone who knows what they are doing and learn from them. Try to enjoy the learning curve. You are acquiring an education that will equip you for the future and make your unique shtick even more unique.

By the way, remember when we tackled demo production back in chapter three? The same principles of networking and bartering apply to website design. If you are a novice at the Internet, approach a local college (or even a high school) arts department. You'll find many young, hip and hungry students who would be delighted to help design a website for you at little or no cost since it gives them an opportunity to develop their portfolio for later employment. Or you may be able to barter them guitar lessons for their work on your site.

Is It A Good Idea to Offer Free Downloads Of My Songs?

Absolutely!

Legendary songwriter Janis Ian makes this point so eloquently in a recent article in *USA Today*:

> *…Consider my experience: I'm a recording artist who hasn't sold multiple platinum records since the 1970s. My site, www.janisian.com, began offering free downloads in July of 2001. About a thousand people per day have downloaded my music, most of them people who had never heard of me and never bought my CDs.*
>
> *On the first day I posted downloadable music, my merchandise sales tripled and they have stayed that way ever since. I'm not about to become a zillionaire as a result, but I am making more money. At a time when radio playlists are tighter and any kind of exposure is hard to come by, 365,000 copies of my work now will be heard. Even if only 3 percent of those people come to concerts or buy my CDs, I've gained about 10,000 new fans this year.*
>
> *That's how artists become successful: exposure. Without exposure, no one comes to shows, and no one buys CDs. After 37 years as a recording artist, when people write to tell me that they came to my concert because they downloaded a song and got curious, I am thrilled.[2]*

Don't you just love it when you discover that one of your musical heroes turns out to be a generous and wonderful person to boot? That's how I feel about Janis. Several years ago I had the opportunity of interviewing her for our radio show. I found her gracious, self-effacing and liberal with her songwriting tips. She is a legend among songwriters but she is eager to extend a hand up to aspiring writers climbing the music ladder. I don't know how you feel, but it makes me want to buy her records—all of them! That's the way people will feel about you if you are generous with your fans.

With the advent of the Internet and the many opportunities for self-promotion it has opened, more and more artists and songwriters are choosing independence simply because the profit margins are so much greater. While they may sell fewer CDs overall, they are still making good money and are able to do the music they love full time. When they are savvy and plan well, they have money for future recordings—and they have creative control over the projects they record (an enviable position for any creative soul)!

To Summarize

Perhaps I can summarize by suggesting that musical success in the twenty-first century will bear little resemblance to the established and accepted concepts of the past. Songwriters and musicians today are de-glamorizing. They are shelving the dream of being bankrolled by benevolent cash cows—otherwise known as record labels. That's the stuff of fantasy! Selling music in the twenty-first century will be like selling any other commodity or product—from mousetraps to mittens.

Question: How will singers and songwriters be distributing music in the years ahead?
Answer: However they can!

Remember: If you are creative, there is no such place as "Nowhere." It's NOW and HERE!

REWIND...

~ A successful song is one that connects with the hearts of listeners.

~ If you're creative enough to write new and original songs, you're creative enough to find new and original ways to distribute them.

~ Successful and innovative strategies are usually not "out there somewhere," but right under your nose.

~ Remain open and teachable. Stay up-to-date on the latest phenomena in music distribution— artist websites, house concerts and the like.

~ Try things. Who knows? They just might work.

[1] ©Vicki Logan/Used by Permission

[2] Janis Ian, *Music Industry Spins Falsehood*, USA Today, October 23, 2002

NOTES

12

Setting Goals and Opening Doors

So Where Exactly Is It That I'm Going In The Music Business?

Excellent question! Especially since you're almost at the end of a book called *How to Get SomeWHERE in the Music Business from Nowhere with Nothing.*

Defining Your Personal Success Quotient

There may well be as many definitions of *success* as there are songwriters and artists in the world. The dictionary defines it as *a favorable result or the attaining of a desired object* or *end*. That's pretty non-specific. It is up to each of us to determine what the favorable result or desired end is going to be.

As we saw in chapter eight, every person has a completely unique shtick or set of talents. Each of us also has what I am inclined to call a *unique success quotient*. This is just another way of saying that what one person considers happiness and success may quite fail to satisfy someone else. Many aspiring artists never identify their unique shtick, and many more never pause to ask what success really means to them.

But Success Means Becoming Rich And Famous, Right?

Not necessarily.

Artists who dominate the media exert a powerful influence on the way we view success. We watch them being cheered by fans as they arrive in limos to attend electrifying award shows, dressed to kill in Versace eveningwear and dripping with jewels. We stare slack-jawed as they mingle nonchalantly with other glittering celebrities (very skinny ladies and broad shouldered hunks) and then radiantly walk the red carpet to receive their prizes. We follow their million dollar weddings and their multi-million dollar breakups. They seem to emerge unscathed to find still more glamorous relationships, even greater financial achievement. And we assume that this is success. They *look* so happy!

Only don't be dazzled by the illusion. Don't be so naïve! We have all heard the horror stories too—the scandals that destroy the lives of even the most talented and celebrated stars. Although success is the dream of most aspiring artists, many of those who make it are hopelessly unprepared for the tidal wave of worry and strain that comes with it. As professions go, the music business is more riddled with tragedies than most. Its successes are so often those who have gained the world and lost themselves in the process. Few of us pause to think it all through before the fact.

So How Do I Avoid These Pitfalls As I Pursue My Dreams?

Accept Responsibility

Whether improving your craft as a songwriter, creating professional demos, learning to act as your own publisher, discovering your unique shtick, or taking advantage of the incredible new opportunities available to artists and writers today—*it all comes down to you*. This is the main theme of our book and a point I have repeated tirelessly, in case you hadn't noticed.

I am always amazed at the many songwriters I meet who have absolutely no idea where they are headed with their music. They love the exhilaration of writing songs so they continue to write them—hoping that somehow, some way, someone will discover them and make them instantly famous. The reality is more in keeping with what one famous artist said when asked how it felt to be an overnight success: "It sure was a hell of a long night!"

He was obviously thinking of the many years of blood, sweat and tears that had gone before. Waiting for someone else to create success and ultimate happiness for you is the stuff of co-dependency not competency. I believe it was Abraham Lincoln who once said, "Most folks are as happy as they make up their minds to be." A more contemporary rendition has it that "happiness is an inside job." These pithy sayings are just different ways of making the point that happiness and personal success come from within and have more to do with our choices than we might be inclined to believe. Here's the question again:

**Are you willing to take responsibility
for your own success…your own happiness?
Have you discovered
your personal success quotient?**

OK, I'm Willing. How Do I Discover My Personal Success Quotient?

Write Away

I encourage anyone who has made it all the way to this chapter of the book to do some serious thinking about what real success means to you. I am a believer in the benefits of journaling. Someone once wisely said: "Thoughts untangle themselves through the fingertips." When you write, you provide yourself an opportunity to explore emotions and ideas that would never otherwise emerge to view. Make some time to be alone. Bring your journal or legal pad and be ready to start writing as you read this chapter.

Bear in mind there are no right answers. Only you can determine what is right for you. I am, however, going to raise some questions as we think this important matter through. You may have to take some breaks, do some thinking and then some more writing, but isn't that what songwriters do anyway? Here are some starters:

- ♫ *Describe your three best memories.*

- ♫ *Thoughtfully analyze those memories. What made them so special? What are the common denominators?*

- ♫ *Describe your three greatest music aspirations or goals.*

- ♫ *If you achieve these objectives, how will they enhance your life specifically? How will they benefit others?*

- ♫ *Specify an income you consider sufficient, even plentiful. What would you do with the surplus if your earnings should exceed that amount?*

- ♫ *What activities, relationships or principles are you unwilling to part with at any price?*

Money Matters

Some of us hope to make millions as songwriters or artists. Others of us may wish we just had enough money to do our music full time and still be able to eat. Wherever money enters your personal success quotient, here are some findings to consider:

> *In a recent study entitled, "Would You Be Happier If You Were Richer?", five renowned professors from four prestigious universities concluded that what your mother always told you is right. It seems that money really can't buy happiness.*

> *The study was conducted by Dr. Alan Krueger and Nobel Laureate Dr. Daniel Kahneman of Princeton University, together with colleagues Dr. David Schkade of the University of California, Dr. Norbert Schwarz of the University of Michigan and Dr. Arthur Stone of New York's Stony Brook University. They surveyed people from all income levels asking questions like—"All things considered, how satisfied are you with your life as a whole these days? Or—"Taken all together would you say that you are very happy, pretty happy or not too happy?"[1]*

Predictably, they found a diminished happiness factor among people with very low annual household incomes (under $20,000) compared with those earning higher incomes ($90,000 or more). But the really startling discovery was this:

**Once a household income reached $50,000
its happiness factor was nearly
indistinguishable from that of households
with incomes exceeding $90,000.**

How on earth could this be true? The scientists postulate:

"Happiness is less dependent on actual income than on relative income— in other words, it's more important to us how we rank financially compared to others in our society."[1] It seems that well-being has more to do with our keeping up with the Joneses than with real dollars and cents.

"Material goods yield little joy for most individuals. Thus, increases in income, which are expected to raise well-being by raising consumption opportunities may in fact have little lasting effect…because the consumption of material goods has little effect on well-being above a certain level."[2] That is, while it is fun and exciting to purchase a new item, the high is too short-lived to seriously impact personal happiness.

As income increases, people tend to devote more time to activities like commuting, childcare, shopping and exercising. Less time is available for real leisure and relaxation. The professors conclude, "The activities that higher-income individuals spend relatively more of their time engaged in are associated with no greater happiness, on average, but with slightly higher tension and stress."[3]

In less scholarly language, desire creates pressure and often anxiety. The time spent acquiring stuff and hanging on to it means less time to really enjoy it. Realistically, you can only drive one car at a time, live in one house at a time, wear one outfit at a time. The rest is just stuff—stuff that rusts, wears out, depreciates faster than the speed of sound, gets stolen, gets old and becomes obsolete. It's overhead that needs to be insured, maintained and stored.

The Fame Fantasy

Fame too has its downside. Before you decide to settle for nothing less than superstardom, consider the high price many pay for it. Celebrities become the targets of salacious tabloid gossip and vicious rumormongering. They live lives without privacy. They (and their families) are hunted and harassed by paparazzi. Their clothes and physical appearance are pitilessly scrutinized and lampooned. They are surrounded by people with self-serving agendas eager to take advantage of them.

Above all there is the matter of *expectations*. When an artist really "makes it" with a brilliant album or blockbuster hit, expectations tend to run high. Sometimes ludicrously high. The artist becomes the subject of great anticipation among her fans, in the media and at her own record label. Will she be able to do it again? Or will she be a one-hit wonder? As she ages, will she remain marketable? Or will the constant influx of new and talented younger artists erode her popularity? The nineteenth century poet, Emily Dickinson said it best:

"Fame is a bee. It has a song. It has a sting. Ah, too, it has a wing."

Assessing the Essentials

Are you still pondering the matter of success? I sure hope so because there's one more very important thing to think over—it is perhaps the most important thing.

Where does art and music fit into
your concept of success?

Your first response to this question may be shock. Success in music is what it's all about, right? But think carefully before you answer. What drives your music? Is it the songs you write...the songs you play...the songs you sing? Are you motivated by dreams of success and fame—or are you motivated by music itself?

A good litmus test for your real motivation is the amount of time you spend actually doing music. Here are a few more questions to answer as you journal:

- ♫ *What great songwriters have you studied recently?*

- ♫ *How many songs have you written in the last three months?*

- ♫ *How many times have you re-written them?*

- ♫ *Have you invested time and money in books and seminars that help improve your craftsmanship as a writer? As an artist?*

- ♫ *Would you be able to stop writing songs if you never made the first dime in profits or royalties? (By the way, if your answer to this question is "yes," you only think you are a songwriter.)*

Many of history's greatest artistic geniuses never achieved in their lifetimes the financial or personal recognition their art deserved. Wolfgang Mozart was a musical prodigy whose compositions are considered the artistic equivalents of Copernicus' revolutionary scientific discoveries. Yet throughout his life he struggled financially. Though he may not have ended in a paupers' grave as legend has suggested, it is true that he died in debt and was buried so modestly that the place he was interred is unknown to this day.

Or consider Michelangelo. Though he was primarily a sculptor, his lifetime love affair with art compelled him to excel at every artistic challenge he was given—from the painting of the magnificent frescoes on the ceiling of the Sistine Chapel to the architecture of St. Peter's in Rome. Throughout his life the great artist was beset with financial and domestic difficulties, poor health, and bitter artistic and political rivalries. Yet, he kept working…all the way up to the time of his death at eighty-nine years of age. It has been said that in the last years of his life he sketched himself as an old man with a telling inscription below the drawing: *ancora impara* (still learning).

Artists like Mozart and Michelangelo were not superhuman. They sought recognition and reward just like we all do. They faced the same difficulties that everyone faces—problems with finances, relationships and illness. But something in them overcame their human frailties—a *restlessness for excellence in every aspect of their art*. The result of their lives and work changed the world forever.

It all comes back to you right here and right now.

♪ *What is the favorable result that defines real success for you?*

♪ *What is your personal success quotient?*

♪ *Are you willing to accept responsibility to achieve it?*

Wow, Kinda Heavy Stuff...What Practical Steps Can I Take?

Live By Your Goals

It has been said that if you aim at nothing, you will be sure to hit it.

When you float through life with hazy objectives, months and years slip away with no observable progress. Think about it: how many talented people do you know who will never be able to give up their day jobs? Why do so few ever achieve their dreams? They may be spinning their wheels in a blur of busyness, but only digging themselves into a rut.

> *Any action that is not based upon a clear, measurable objective tends to become activity without productivity—the end result is usually bitterness and burnout.*

Long-Range Goals

Having pondered the matters of money, fame, music and success, it is now time to write out your long-range music goal. Where do you want to be ten years from now? What do you want to be doing? What do you hope to accomplish?

Now, let me be the first to say that your long-range goal may need to be modified many times along the way. In chapter eight we discussed the importance of allowing life and music to guide you as your path unfolds. It is nevertheless imperative that you articulate a clear music objective, one that accurately reflects your success quotient. A working definition will help orient you. It will get you moving and keep you going.

It is essential that your objective be clear, concise and measurable. Refrain from using vague and ambiguous language. Make it as specific as possible. Here are some examples of poorly and well-written long-range goals:

♪ **Poorly Written Long-Range Goal:**
My goal is to become rich and successful as a songwriter. (What exactly is "rich" and what is "successful"?)

♪ **Well-Written Long-Range Goal:**
My goal is to be able to comfortably support my family on my music income alone while maintaining creative control of my music catalog and at least 25% of the publisher's share of each song.

Short-Range Goals

Short-range goals are usually easier to achieve and can become milestones on the road to success. They provide motivation and encouragement as you move ahead. The more short-range ventures you attempt, the more competent you will become in a variety of skills. Each new skill becomes another opportunity for success and every success becomes part of your ever-expanding Success Resume.

Write at least three immediate
short-range goals that you can complete
within the next three months.

These may be baby steps. That's all right. You could start by assuming the mentoring role of the publisher and put yourself on a songwriting regimen as suggested in chapter one. You might decide to read two books on the craft or business of songwriting and set a deadline for finishing those books. You might do an Internet study on house concerts and attend one near you. Maybe you'll decide to sign up for a website design course at your local community college. Or you could perform a searching and fearless inventory to discover your unique shtick as suggested in chapter eight.

Whichever short-range objectives you set, keep them in line with your long-range objective, and be sure that they are clear, concise and measurable. Include a timetable for the activities you undertake to ensure you are not just fooling yourself. Here are some examples:

♪ **Poorly Written Short-Range Goal:**
I will learn more about songwriting this year
(What is "more"? When and how will you learn it?)

♪ **Well-Written Short-Range Goal:**
I will work through the course called "Successful Lyric Writing" by Sheila Davis. I will accomplish this by spending one hour studying each Monday and Thursday evening from 7:00 to 8:00 PM. On this schedule I will have completed the course by March 15.

When you have completed the first set of short-range objectives, move on to something a little more challenging. Perhaps you'll begin pitching songs to artists in your area…or perform at your own house concert. You might volunteer to help write this year's Christmas musical at your church or decide to audit a recording session by a local artist to learn the basics of sound engineering. With each new objective, you will be building musical muscle, increasing your skills and establishing your credibility.

Don't spread yourself too thin or lose track of what you are doing in your pursuit of short-range goals. Each one should be a measurable step toward your final destination. Success is a combustible thing. Achievement in one area of your career will quickly spread to others—until all your efforts are on fire with success. A broad foundation in many skills will help you to adjust your long-range goal as you grow, and equip you to handle ultimate success when it arrives.

But All This Seems So Mechanical...Won't Discipline Stifle My Talent and Creativity?

Oh, how right-brained we songwriters are!

We are so afraid of murdering the Muse that we resist anything that smacks of discipline or structure. God forbid someone suggest a re-write of our latest divinely inspired song! And words like *scheduling*, *accountability* and *consistency?* Well, they go against every spontaneous, free-spirited instinct we possess! The truth is, however, that without discipline, we remain flakier than pie dough.

You may be the mother lode of raw musical talent, but without a proper balance of time-tested business principles you may never escape the ranks of the undiscovered and obsolete. Consider these fundamentals...

An Open Mind

Every creative person owes it to herself to consider new ideas and perspectives. This has never been truer than it is now with the New Millennium well underway and technology bringing unprecedented changes. The fact remains that many aspiring artists and songwriters seem nearly incapable of adapting their minds to the realities of music as it is today.

Many harbor the long-entrenched belief that the one and only road to *real* success is to be discovered by a major music company and transformed into an instant sensation. Many live in mortal fear of the very technological advances designed to empower them and open new paths to achievement. I realize that change of any kind can be uncomfortable to process. It is far easier to hide behind a right-brained artistic persona and live in Fantasyland than to keep an open and teachable mind.

Let me assure you: *You will not be compromised by learning new methods or by observing how other gifted songwriters approach the craft and business of songwriting.* A humble and inquisitive attitude can only expand your horizons, develop your potential, keep you relevant and make you a more skilled professional.

Commitment

Whether you are just getting started as a songwriter, or have been writing for years, you must review your objectives often and be committed to reaching them—*whatever it takes!* One thing this commitment will surely take is time.

> *Commitment must be translated into time invested for it to mean anything at all.*

What distinguishes a professional from a hobbyist is time—time spent setting and achieving goals. I submit that unless you are willing to spend a minimum of ten to fifteen hours a week developing your skills and realizing your objectives, you will remain something of a dabbler.

For those who still have day jobs, it won't be easy to meet this challenge, but discipline and consistency are crucial if you hope to succeed. Staying committed will require accountability. Plot clearly articulated goals on a realistic timeline—then keep to your schedule. A good way to stay on track is to meet with a close songwriting friend on a regular basis to discuss your goals. Keep one another focused and moving forward!

Realistically, your big break will probably not happen this month—or even six months from now. If it does, you will be pleasantly surprised, but please don't be discouraged if even years go by before you get that cut by a major artist or receive national recognition. It's a day-by-day commitment that bridges the gap between where you are now and where you're headed!

A Generous Spirit

I believe there is a universal spiritual principle that states, "You can't keep what you are unwilling to give away." No matter how low you are on the music food chain, I promise you that there is someone with even less knowledge and experience following close behind. You only have to be one rung higher on the ladder of success to lend a hand up to the person behind you.

Make time in your overcrowded schedule to mentor someone else. Make it a priority. Give guitar lessons to a troubled teenager. Extend a hand of welcome to a newcomer at your songwriters' group. Be willing to really listen to someone else's songs and be ready with a word of encouragement. Remember how much it means to have someone say they believe in you and care.

There are songwriters all over the world who need a boost of hope and help. For several years my colleague, Sarah Marshall, and I have each mentored songwriters in Africa via the Internet. Sarah has a contact in Kenya; I have one in Nigeria. These writers have very few resources and are extremely eager for tools and information about songwriting. Encouraging them is always a blessing to us. As my good friend, Peggy Frank, says: "When you give to others, you are only giving to yourself." Somehow, some way, generosity always comes back to you—multiplied.

Don't let yourself become paranoid, competitive and greedy—no matter how hard your journey or unfair its circumstances. Be happy for other artists' successes! Be large of heart! Nothing is more attractive.

Now That I'm Doing All This...Can I Officially Call Myself A "Professional Songwriter"?

Absolutely.

There is no official test to pass or standard to reach that qualifies you as a pro. If you have identified your objectives and are consistently devoting a portion of your time each week to the pursuit of your goals, I give you my full permission to declare yourself a professional and to begin thinking of yourself that way.

Bear in mind that people you meet in the music industry (local or national) will form an impression of you based on how you communicate yourself to them, and this is intrinsically linked to how you feel about yourself. If you see yourself as a second-class songwriter because you haven't yet had that blockbuster hit, those you meet will tend to see you as inferior. But if you are committed to a standard of excellence in your craft and in your business, you will convey an authentic air of confidence to others. Instead of a dog with a hangdog inferiority complex, you can be a dog who wags his own tail. You can create the impression that you are the best-kept secret in music—a skilled professional and someone others need to know about if they want to be on the cutting edge.

Wow! So How Do I Start Living My New Identity?

Here are a few ideas to get you started:

When asked what you do for a living, instead of saying, "I am a checkout clerk at Wal-Mart," try saying, "I am a songwriter by profession, but at the moment, I also work for the Wal-Mart Corporation."

When you fill out forms at the doctor's office, write "songwriter" or "musician" in the blank where you're asked to state your profession. Then make note of the responses you get from your doctor and others when they see what you have written. More often than not, they will grin and say, "Wow! So you're a songwriter…Cool!" (That's because everyone is secretly a songwriter himself and wishes he were doing what you are doing.)

> I'll never forget an experience I had at a venture capital luncheon in a large hotel. Most of the attendees were three-piece-suit-dot-com executives—and rather stuffy to say the least. As we went around the table introducing ourselves, each gentleman identified himself by his profession—computer specialist, Internet marketing director etc. When it came to me, the only female at the table, I said, "I'm Mary Dawson and I'm a songwriter." You should have seen the expressions on their faces. My stock went up about 100 points! Go ahead…try it! You'll see what I mean.

Begin to develop a persona in keeping with your new identity and your music. You may want to begin dressing a little more creatively or wearing your hair in a more imaginative style. A good example of this is the evolution of the legendary singer-songwriter, Willie Nelson. When Willie first began his career, photographs reveal that he looked and dressed more like an accountant than a musician. But look at him now! He has certainly developed his own unique persona!

Why the emphasis on identity? Is it really that important? You may or may not choose to apply the suggestions above, but your self-concept is essential. It will influence how you present yourself in person, over the Internet and on the telephone as you seek to contact people within the industry. It will also affect how your own music community perceives you. If you see yourself as a clerk, a housewife, a plumber or a doctor, you will not have the assertiveness or persistence required to play the part of a professional songwriter. And this can make a world of difference!

Is This What You Call Faking It Till You Make It?

Yep! It's a powerful and effective technique. But be ready to have your bluff called, at least from time to time. Here's one of my own favorite stories…

My office has always been in my home. It began in a corner of my sewing room but as the years passed and my company grew, I acquired a full-blown office/studio with my own business phone. For convenience, we have two-line telephones all over the house. If line one rings, we know it is for CQK Music or I Write the Songs. If line two rings, we know it's for a member of the family.

One morning as I was having breakfast, my business line rang. "CQK Music," I answered. On the line was a songwriter from South Dakota. She asked if she might submit some songs to be considered for publication. I started into my usual spiel about how we were a very small company and rarely signed outside material. Suddenly the songwriter interrupted me. She said, "Yeah, I can tell you guys are a really small outfit."

"Really," I said. "How do you know?"
"Because I just heard your toaster pop!" she answered.

My cover was BLOWN!!!

…which bring us to a very important point. To survive what may be a long and winding road to success you have to be having fun along the way. So if you don't already have one, develop a sense of humor. *The journey is the end in this business.* If you become road-weary and you're no longer having fun, it's time to re-examine the whole gig and decide whether to make some procedural adjustments—you may even need to change your long-range goals. A music career at any level is fraught with rejection and difficulty. You will meet some wonderful people along the way, but you will also meet some real jerks. A good sense of humor will help you roll with the punches. Learn to laugh and move on.

The End Of This Book Is Only The Beginning, Right?

Right!

Don't just finish reading this book and put it up on a shelf. Begin planning the 1.5—2 hour per day commitment required. Whatever your greatest need is now, take steps to meet it. You will soon find that you are getting somewhere in the music business one day, one adventure at a time.

And don't stop. No matter how small the steps you take, no matter how difficult the road, stay the course and press on!

> *Remember: The greatest thing you can do to build credibility is simply to survive.*

Think about that for a moment. Think about all the singers, movie stars, musicians, record labels and television shows that enjoyed a modicum of success and then simply vanished. When their fifteen minutes of fame was up, they were never heard from again. You may be small and not quite as flashy, but you keep plugging along. Those that dismissed you yesterday will eventually figure out you intend to stay. They will realize that where others have come and gone, you are still standing. You're still on the radar, tracking forward.

You Can't Lose If You Don't Quit

I once heard a story about a swimmer who wanted to be the first woman to swim the twenty-six miles from the California coast to Catalina Island. On the morning of her swim a dense fog set in. As she swam, the weather got worse. She soon became very cold and stiff and began to suspect she would not be able to continue. Her support team in the boat beside her encouraged her to keep swimming, but she finally got so cold and discouraged that she gave up and climbed into the boat. At that moment the fog lifted and she saw the coast of Catalina Island just 100 feet off. She had given up a little too soon. Don't let this happen to you!

Right in front of the desk in my office is a beautiful picture of a river running through a rocky, mountainous area. A tree seems to be growing right up out of the rock along the river. The caption beneath the picture reads:

> **PERSEVERANCE**: *In the confrontation between the stream and the rock, the stream always wins, not through strength but through persistence.*[4]

See you at the Grammys!

REWIND...

~ Identify your personal success quotient.

~ Write clear, concise, measurable long-range and short-range goals.

~ Practice open-mindedness, commitment and generosity on a daily basis.

~ Claim your identity as a professional songwriter.

~ Maintain a good sense of humor and enjoy the journey.

Never, Never Quit!

[1] Daniel Kahneman, Alan B. Krueger, David Schkade, Norbert Schwarz, Arthur A. Stone; *Would You Be Happier If You Were Richer? A Focusing Illusion*, Science Magazine, Vol.312, No. 5782; pp. 1908-1910

[2] Ibid

[3] Ibid

[4] H. Jackson Brown

NOTES

EPILOGUE

Believe it or not, I have been writing this book for almost ten years now. It's hard to realize that it's finished at last—or maybe "ended" is a better word. (Is any song or any book ever really finished?).

It started out as a forty-page manual answering basic questions I receive from aspiring songwriters through my Internet radio show, *I Write the Songs*, and through my music publishing companies. To keep pace with the swift and titanic changes occurring in the music industry I was compelled to re-think, re-structure, and re-write that manual so often that it gradually morphed into the book you have been reading. I hope it has given you food for thought.

Paradigms Really Do Change

You don't have to be as old as I am to remember an era several decades ago when smoking was considered cool. Cigarette companies sponsored some of the best TV programs on the air and tobacco was considered a great American industry. Everyone smoked…our favorite movie stars, successful business-men, the really hip kids in high school—everybody.

Eventually a few non-specific warnings were issued. The surgeon general cautioned that *smoking may be hazardous to your health*. They put a little notice on cigarette packs, but no one really paid attention to it. The nation continued to smoke—just as it always had. Cigarette companies continued making millions.

But as the years passed we heard more and more about diseases caused by smoking—heart disease, cancer, and emphysema. The warnings on cigarette packs became more urgent. The surgeon general began insisting cigarettes were harmful. Cigarette ads were banned on television, and the Marlboro man died of lung cancer. We soon had smoking and non-smoking sections in restaurants and on airplanes. Victims of smoke-related diseases began bringing lawsuits against cigarette companies and winning. Times were changing. Smoking was not so cool anymore.

Last week at Midway International Airport in Chicago I heard this announcement repeated at least half a dozen times on the public address system: *Smoking is completely banned throughout the airport AND within fifty feet of any of the main entrances*. My husband, who had just returned from England, mentioned that some British cigarette packs now carry a notice that reads, *Warning: Cigarettes kill*. That's what you call a paradigm change!

But it didn't happen overnight. We who lived through the tobacco revolution were slow to change our ways. At first, we ignored the warnings. We blamed those alarmists who are always discovering something else that's bad for us. But more and more hard science emerged to view, all of it bad news for smokers. We began to observe first-hand the effects of smoking on our aging parents and to resent the risk cigarettes posed to our children.

Today the unimaginable has happened. Public opinion has done an about-face. Healthier living has become cool. We're eating better, exercising. We're not smoking. After an avalanche of litigation in the late nineties, powerful tobacco companies must now actively discourage smoking among minors and help parents hold the line with legally mandated anti-smoking advertising campaigns and online services. Incredible!

And smoking is just one of several *impossible* paradigm shifts witnessed in the last half-century. Many of us saw the Berlin Wall come down and Apartheid in South Africa toppled. Those of us who are a little older remember the demise of legal segregation in America. We have seen the erosion of racist bigotry in places where it was so entrenched it seemed things would never change. The rise of the Feminist Movement has opened opportunities to women in the workplace unthinkable just thirty years ago.

Yes, paradigms do change but not overnight and the process can be a messy one. Now it is the music paradigm that is changing, and changing radically. We who are living through this momentous transition will need a solid understanding of the old ways of doing business—one animated by a vision of the future that is just around the corner.

One thing is certain: *the era of powerful multi-million dollar companies controlling the music we love is rapidly coming to a close.* Technology and entrepreneurship are instantly disseminating information and opening doors to independent songwriters and artists that have been locked and bolted for decades. The planet has already shifted on its axis and the music of the spheres will never sound quite the same again.

Of course the old music industry continues to exist and do business the old way. There are still artists signing record deals with major labels. Primetime talent shows make people you never heard of into household names—seemingly overnight. Sometimes an independent songwriter actually lands a cut on a major record. But as we have seen, music as a business is on the move— a new era is dawning under different signs.

If I am correct in my estimate, at present we are in a *both-and* stage. It's not time to completely renounce the old paradigm. There is no *either-or* standoff unless we force one, thumbing our noses at the traditionalists. The music industry can be so exasperating at times you may be tempted to do just this. But remember that as an artist your chief responsibility is to keep making good art. Keep all your options open. Make it your aim to be as well-versed and professionally sophisticated in the craft and business of songwriting as anyone in the industry today. Don't burn bridges.

The good news is that we have new choices now. Only a few years ago the prevailing attitude in the music industry was: *We've never heard of you. You must not be any good.* Today the attitude is less complacent: *We've never heard of you. Maybe we're missing something.*

How do we anticipate the new and not lose touch with the old? It may mean learning to act in ways that seem somewhat counterintuitive at first. We may slip and slide before we find our legs. Remember, the winds of change are carrying us to a new world—one that is likely to be far more democratic than the old one. It will probably be less inhibited and more spontaneous too, as artists from every walk of life learn to communicate across continents and cultures. And it's sure to be more spacious, for the old walls will have crumbled, making room for everybody.

Postscript...

Remember Vicki Logan from back in chapter eleven? She's the songwriter from Minnesota whose *Moo-ed Music* had the amazing lactation effect on dairy cows.

In the months since I wrote chapter eleven Vicki has been writing, performing and working every creative angle she can. Her music is currently broadcast on over 1,500 stations. Somehow (and she thinks it had something to do with the Internet) she was noticed by Chi-Lin International, a distributor from Taiwan with offices in California. She has just signed a distribution contract with them for a "Vicki Logan CD" featuring 14 of her original songs. Slated for release in Taiwan, the album's linear notes will all be in Chinese.

Not enough? Check this out...Vicki was recently approached by Spirit Media, a television station in Bulgaria, seeking a license to use her songs as background music for several of their TV programs. And she has been invited to come to Bulgaria for a televised concert.

She has also been busy moving into her beautiful new 7,000 square foot home where she plans to host house concerts. Eight of this year's scheduled concerts will be filmed as a series and broadcast on Forest Lakes TV10, her regional network. In a recent email Vicki wrote: "Life isn't about what perspective everyone else has on it, it's all about *yours* and creating the life that *you* want."

When I called the other day to congratulate Vicki on all her successes, her daughter informed me that her mom couldn't come to the phone just then... she was out mowing the lawn.

Now, that's what I call a New Paradigm!

APPENDIX A

Basic Information on Copyright and Registration with the Library of Congress

The word copyright means simply the exclusive *right to copy, reproduce, publish and sell a literary, musical or artistic work*. For songwriters, the good news is that you really don't have to do anything except write a song in order to be protected by copyright law. Copyright goes into effect automatically the moment the expression of an original idea becomes fixed in a tangible form or medium, as for instance, a written lyric sheet, transcribed notes on music paper, or an audio recording.

Most people in the music business understand copyright law and will not try to steal songs from songwriters. If, however, you are circulating your songs among a wide variety of publishers and record companies, or when you are sending songs or lyrics over the Internet, it is wise to *register your copyrights* formally with the US Copyright Office in Washington, D.C.

Since there is a government form to fill out and a charge for each copyright registration, songwriters frequently resort to what is called the "poor man's copyright." This consists of a recording on tape or CD, or written words and music that a songwriter mails to herself in a sealed, postmarked envelope which she then files unopened as proof of the originality and date of composition. This may help prove the authenticity of your claim to have written the song should it ever be contested, but the United States Copyright Office holds that mailing something to yourself has no legal meaning under copyright law. Each court of law assigns whatever evidentiary weight it thinks fit to documents of this type, which is to say, they may sometimes assign them none at all. It is just as easy and far safer, therefore, to officially register your song(s) with the Copyright Office. And I'm going to show you how to do it cheap—so read on!

The first step is to secure the proper form. Believe it or not, in this particular case the government has actually *simplified* the process. Forms can be easily downloaded at **www.copyright.gov**.

For completed songs or musical works, you will need a *PA Form. PA* stands for *Performing Arts*. For lyrics only or poetry you can use a *TX Form (for Text)*. If you don't have access to the Internet, you can call the Forms Hotline at **202-707-9100**. You will hear a recorded message with instructions for how to request the forms you need. Forms are mailed out free of charge.

For each *PA Form* submitted, there is a registration fee (at the time this book went to press the fee was $45.00 per registration). If you only register one song at a time, this procedure can get very expensive—especially if you are a prolific songwriter. There is, however, a cheaper way!

You can wait until you have several songs ready for registration and then register them as a "collection." The collection can contain any number of songs (my last submission had over 20) and it requires just one registration fee. I title my collections *The Songs of Mary Dawson: Volume 1 (or Volume 2…or Volume 3…*or whatever). You will need to include your completed PA Form along with a cassette or CD demo of the songs in the submission together with lyric sheets for each song. If you prefer, you may submit the songs in written form as lead sheets or scores with lyrics.

Be sure to keep a list of the titles in each collection you register. The individual titles will not appear on the executed registration you receive back from the Copyright Office. If you neglect to keep a list of the titles in each collection, it will be more difficult for you to locate the registration of a specific song in the Copyright Office should you wish to negotiate a songwriter's agreement with a larger publisher or enter into a co-publishing agreement sometime in future.

It takes several months for the registration procedure to be completed, but you will eventually receive your registration certificate in the mail. Be sure to file it in a safe place along with the list of songs in that collection. If and when you decide to sign a songwriter's agreement with a publisher or record company, the copyright for the song(s) in the agreement will have to be re-registered to show transfer of copyright ownership to the publisher. It is, however, a simple matter to re-register the song(s) and it is usually the publisher's responsibility.

If you are a singer/songwriter recording an album of your own songs to sell at concerts or to distribute in some other way, you will need to register the entire recording so that the album as a *whole* is also protected by copyright law. This requires an *SR* (stands for *Sound Recording) Form*. It is a little different than the PA form described above. The symbol for this copyright is the letter P (for *Phonorecord*) in a circle ℗. You will notice this symbol on commercial recordings. It should also appear on any albums you manufacture.

When you digest the above information, you will have a basic working knowledge of copyright. Copyright Law—like any legal statute—is filled with intricacies and fine points that can only be accurately interpreted by specialists in the field. Thankfully, these specialists can be reached easily by phone at the Copyright Office. I have found them extremely helpful and ready to answer questions. *The Real Human Being Hotline Number* is: **202-707-5959**.

Don't be overwhelmed by copyright registration. If you are faithful to mark your songs with the proper copyright notice and to register them regularly with the US Copyright Office, you can freely hoist your sails and cruise the seas of the music business in the knowledge that "the Law is on your side" and will protect your songs from song pirates.

APPENDIX B

EXAMPLE OF A POORLY-WRITTEN LYRIC SHEET

Font is artistic, but almost totally illegible.

Title is not bolded

Rhymes and rhyme schemes are completely lost by lines that are too long

Chorus and Bridge are not labeled and set apart – difficult to locate at first glance

I LOVE TO LOOK AT YOU

There are faces that I never tire of seeing and smiles that never fail to warm my heart
There are places that I never tire of being though miles and memories keep us apart
Whether we are really here alone together or you're simply in my mind where I remember.....

I love to look at you, I love to trace your face with my eyes
And I can't disguise the truth, I'm hypnotized by your every move
O, Baby, I love to look at you

They say beauty's in the eye of the beholder and I know very well that saying's true
Cause my feelings just don't change as we grow older and beauty's still another word for you
So let me feast my eyes and fill my senses for I only see you through a lover's lenses

I know that you can't see how beautiful you really are
But, Baby, please believe me, what I say comes from my heart......

Words and Music by Mary Dawson
Copyright © 2002/CQK Music
Phone: 111-111-1111, Fax: 111-111-1112
Email: info@emailaddress.com

EXAMPLE OF A POORLY-WRITTEN LYRIC SHEET WITH MORE LEGIBLE FONT

Title is still not bolded

I LOVE TO LOOK AT YOU

Lines are still far too long – rhymes and rhyme scheme are lost

There are faces that I never tire of seeing and smiles that never fail to warm my heart
There are places that I never tire of being though miles and memories keep us apart
Whether we are really here alone together or you're simply in my mind where I remember.....

I love to look at you, I love to trace your face with my eyes
And I can't disguise the truth, I'm hypnotized by your every move
O, Baby, I love to look at you

Chorus and Bridge are still not labeled correctly

They say beauty's in the eye of the beholder and I know very well that saying's true
Cause my feelings just don't change as we grow older and beauty's still another word for you
So let me feast my eyes and fill my senses for I only see you through a lover's lenses

I know that you can't see how beautiful you really are
But, Baby, please believe me, what I say comes from my heart......

Words and Music by Mary Dawson
Copyright © 2002/CQK Music
Phone: 111-111-1111
Fax:111-111-1112
Email: info@emailaddress.com

BUT LOOK WHAT A LEGIBLE FONT CAN DO!!!!
(See next page)

230

EXAMPLE OF A WELL-WRITTEN LYRIC SHEET

Letterhead provides all essential contact information, including address and phone number

CQK Records & Music

Mary Dawson
Address, Suite A, City, State, Zip Code
Phone: 111-111-1111 • Fax 111-111-1112

Title is in bold print

I LOVE TO LOOK AT YOU

Rhymes and rhyme patterns are indicated by the layout of each line

There are faces that I never tire of seeing
And smiles that never fail to warm my heart
There are places that I never tire of being
Though miles and memories keep us apart
Whether we are really here alone together
Or you're simply in my mind where I remember.....

Chorus and Bridge are in bold print and easy to locate

CHORUS: I love to look at you
I love to trace your face with my eyes
And I can't disguise the truth
I'm hypnotized by your every move
O, Baby, I love to look at you.

They say beauty's in the eye of the beholder
And I know very well that saying's true
Cause my feelings just don't change as we grow older
And beauty's still another word for you
So let me feast my eyes and fill my senses
For I only see you through a lover's lenses

BRIDGE: I know that you can't see
How beautiful you really are
But, Baby, please believe me
What I say comes from my heart......

Font is clear, legible, and a good point size which is easy to read

(usually 10 to 12 point type on a full-size document)

Words and Music by Mary Dawson
Copyright © 2002/CQK Music
Phone: 111-111-1111
Fax: 111-111-1112
Email: info@emailaddress.com

GUIDES FOR A
WELL-WRITTEN COVER LETTER

TIPS:

- *Brevity* is the key word when it comes to writing cover letters.

  When you are introduced to someone for the first time, you simply shake her hand and say, "I'm pleased to meet you." You don't give her your complete personal history, or even your business resume. You simply make contact. That's the way to think about a cover letter; *it's an introduction on paper*. A cover letter should rarely, if ever, be longer than one page.

- Use your carefully designed letterhead (see chapter four)

- Use proper business letter format.

  Be sure your letter includes:

  - Date
  - Name and address of recipient
  - Salutation
  - Proper complimentary close
  - Signature
  - Printed name of sender below signature
  - Initials of sender and secretary

- Refer to the person you contacted by phone or email

  Remember our rule from chapter ten: NEVER send any submission (by mail or by MP3) without first having made personal contact with someone and obtaining permission to send it.

EXAMPLE OF A
WELL-WRITTEN COVER LETTER*

Date

Bollingsworth M. Bigshot
Brand X Records
555 Record Contract Blvd.
Hollywood, CA 90027

Dear Mr. Bigshot:

This letter is a follow-up to my conversation earlier today with your secretary,
Mitzi, who gave me permission to send a few of my songs for you to review.

Please find enclosed lyric sheets and a demo CD for three songs:

> ***Above the Clouds*** – An R&B/pop dance tune that may be
> appropriate for the new Aretha Holly project scheduled for
> recording later this year.

> ***Private Collection*** – a Country/Blues ballad

> ***Walking Through the Storm*** – An uptempo Bluegrass Gospel
> song that may be of interest to your new male Gospel
> vocalist, Hal A. Luya. I understand that he is gathering songs
> for his first project.

Thanks for listening.

Sincerely,

Star Wannabe

Star Wannabe

SW/ms
enclosures

**Don't have a secretary?
Hey, I've used my kid's or even
my dog's initials here. Necessity
is the mother of invention.**

APPENDIX C

LETTER OF AGREEMENT FOR CO-WRITERS

Co-writers often avoid drawing up agreements between them because they fear it will involve excessive legal expenses they can't afford. So they opt for doing nothing—hoping there will never be a problem. A simple letter of agreement provides a workable alternative. It is a very simple contract—a *written handshake*. If signed by all parties, it is considered a binding legal agreement and recognized as such even if it is written on spiral notebook paper.

**No matter how simply stated
an agreement may be, *something* on paper is always better
than *nothing* on paper.**

Letters of agreement among co-writers do not threaten relationships; they confirm and clarify them. Most co-writing projects are joined in a spirit of friendship and creativity. As time and relationships change, the letter of agreement serves to refresh the memories of all involved in the good faith creation of a song. *The palest ink is better than the most retentive memory.*

TIPS:

- **State the Agreement Simply**

  This letter is intended to document plainly what the co-writers have agreed to verbally.

- **Make a copy of the letter for each of the writers.**

- **Be sure all copies are signed by all writers** (no photocopies of signatures).

- **Make an extra copy to be placed in a safe deposit box or with a trusted party.**

- **The sample letter on the next page is very basic and may be adapted as required. More detailed templates may be designed by consulting music resources such as:**

    - *The Musicians Business and Legal Guide* (a presentation of the Beverly Hills Bar Association) www.bhba.org

    - http://www.johnbraheny.com/bus/index.html

EXAMPLE OF CO-WRITER AGREEMENT*

Date

This letter of agreement outlines our ownership of the song entitled *I'm Sorry, Dear, I Made You Cry but Now Your Face is Clean* (the Composition). The co-authors of the Composition are:

Anita Hitt
Carrie Oakey
Phil Mypockets

The co-authors agree to share equally 100% of the Writers' Share as follows:

Anita Hitt – 33 1/3%
Carrie Oakey – 33 1/3%
Phil Mypockets – 33 1/3%

The co-authors agree to share equally 100% of the Publisher's Share as follows:

Anita Hitt – 33 1/3 %
Carrie Oakey – 33 1/3 %
Phil Mypockets – 33/1/3%

Co-authors will share equally expenses incurred to produce a professional demo of the Composition, to promote and pitch the Composition for profit and to register the copyright with the Library of Congress.

Co-authors will share equally in any income generated by their mutual efforts according to the percentages agreed to above.

All co-authors shall have the right to issue licenses for any use of the song, but must pay appropriate shares of any income received to the other co-authors.

Signatures below indicate compliance with this agreement.

Anita Hitt	Social Security Number
Carrie Oakey	Social Security Number
Phil Mypockets	Social Security Number

+ **Several songs may be covered by one agreement if the percentages and points of ownership are the same.** In this case, simply add a page at the end of the agreement called *Schedule A*, listing all compositions to be included. Then, replace the first sentence of the letter above with the following:

> *This letter of agreement outlines our ownership of the songs listed in Schedule A of this document (the Compositions).*

Letter of Agreement with Demo Producer

A letter of agreement with the demo producer is especially important when a songwriter is engaging the services of a producer for the first time. As with the co-writers' agreement, this letter is simply a *written handshake*— clarifying the verbal agreement reached previously.

Review carefully the suggestions in chapter three, *The Demo*, before rushing into demo production. Remember that if you have composed *words and melody*, you are the author of a song. You will pay the demo producer to *arrange and produce* your song in an audio recording. Most demo producers contract with songwriters on a *work-for-hire* basis, meaning that they are compensated for their services in a one-time payment. They do not ordinarily receive a percentage of the writers' or publishers' share of the copyright.

Be absolutely sure that both you and your prospective producer are in agreement before you begin the production in order to prevent misunderstandings later.

TIPS:

- ♦ **Make a rough demo of your song(s)—a cappella if necessary— prior to your first session with a new demo producer. Register rough demos with the US Copyright Office (see Appendix A).**

- ♦ **Review and sign the letter of agreement with the producer before your first session.**

- ♦ **Make an extra copy of the agreement to be placed in a safe deposit box or with a trusted party.**

- ♦ **Several song demos may be covered by one letter of agreement as long as the production components and fees are the same for each title.**

Example of a
Letter of Agreement with Demo Producer*

Date

Pete Producer
Pete's Professional Productions
555 Allegro Circle
Boondocks, Montana 59801

This is a letter of agreement between Pete Producer and Melody Tune outlining our working relationship.

Schedule A, which is attached to this letter, records the titles of songs (Compositions) that will be produced as demo recordings by Pete Producer and Pete's Professional Productions as works for hire (as such term is defined by Copyright Law) and all rights to the songs are the sole property of Melody Tune as author of the songs.

Melody Tune agrees to pay Pete Producer and Pete's Professional Productions $_____ for each demo produced of the Compositions on *Schedule A*. Payment for each master will be made prior to acquisition.

Pete Producer and Pete's Professional Productions will retain no ownership percentage of the copyrights. Melody Tune agrees to use demos produced by Pete Producer and Pete's Professional Productions for promotional purposes only and will not use any artist's name or likeness to promote the song. Demos will not be sold. *Schedule A* attached to this letter will record the titles of songs covered by this agreement and may be amended by initialing of both parties as songs are added to the production list.

Signatures below indicate compliance with this agreement.

Accepted and Agreed

By:_____   _____
          Melody Tune   Social Security Number

By:_____   _____
       Peter R. Producer   Social Security or Federal I.D. Number

---

* The above sample letter of agreement is for illustration only. The author shall not be responsible for any reproduction of this agreement for personal or business use.